THE STORY OF
BUILDINGS

For my mother, who loves buildings too – PD

To Liz and Richard – SB

First published 2014 by Walker Books Ltd, 87 Vauxhall Walk, London SE11 5HJ • 10 9 8 7 6 5 4 3 2 1 • Text © 2014 Patrick Dillon • Illustrations © 2014 Stephen Biesty • The right of Patrick Dillon and Stephen Biesty to be identified as author and illustrator respectively of this work has been asserted by them in accordance with the Copyright, Designs and Patents Act 1988 • This book has been typeset in Futura and Adobe Caslon • Printed in China • All rights reserved. No part of this book may be reproduced, transmitted or stored in an information retrieval system in any form or by any means, graphic, electronic or mechanical, including photocopying, taping and recording, without prior written permission from the publisher. • British Library Cataloguing in Publication Data: a catalogue record for this book is available from the British Library • ISBN 978-1-4063-3590-3 • **www.walker.co.uk**

THE STORY OF BUILDINGS
WORLD ARCHITECTURE FROM THE PYRAMIDS TO THE POMPIDOU CENTRE

Written by PATRICK DILLON • Illustrated by STEPHEN BIESTY

WALKER BOOKS
AND SUBSIDIARIES
LONDON • BOSTON • SYDNEY • AUCKLAND

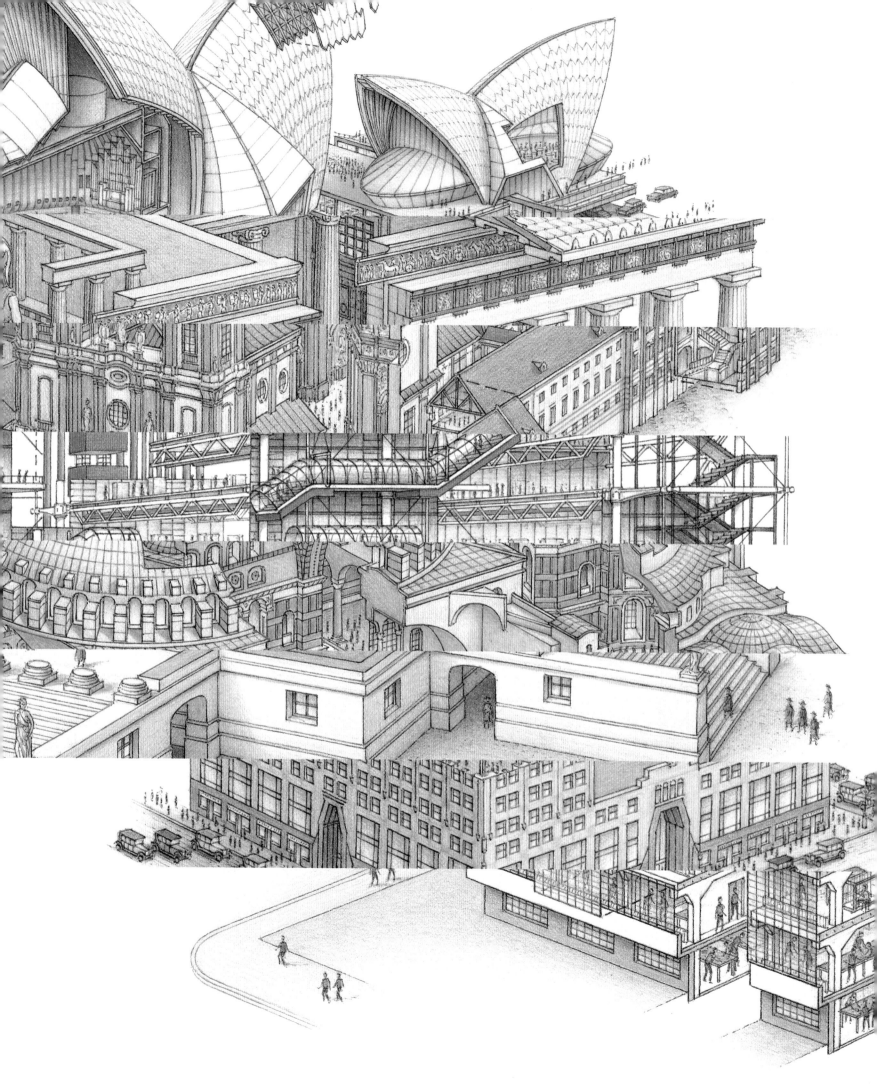

CONTENTS

BUILDING A HOUSE

Imagine you find yourself in a forest. Night is falling. You have to build a shelter.

You gather sticks and stack them up to make a cabin, but the sticks keep toppling over. At last you learn how to tie them with creepers to hold them upright, but when you crawl into the cabin there's hardly any space inside. Logs don't keep out the rain either. It trickles between them and drips on your face.

Maybe you find yourself in the mountains, so you decide to make a stone house. But though you gather all the stones you can find, you don't have anything to stick them together with. After hours of hard work your house is just a heap of rocks.

If you find yourself by a river, it's even worse: there's nothing to build with but mud. You squeeze out the water and pat it into shape, but as the rising sun dries it, long cracks appear and your walls collapse in a cloud of dust.

In the end you decide to find a shelter that's already there, so you look for a cave.

And that's what the first people did. They didn't have tools strong enough to shape wood or cut rock. They didn't know how to glue stone or stiffen clay. So whenever they could, they made their homes in caves.

Now look around you at the house you live in. Maybe you live in a brick house in the country with a tall roof rising above the trees. Maybe you live on an estate in a city and your windows look across miles of roofs and chimneys, squares and streets. Maybe you live on a farm or by the sea, in a flat over a shop, or a house down a side road. Wherever you live, you probably have heating to keep you warm in winter, a bathroom with taps that gush hot and cold water, and electric lights so you can read at night. It's miles better than growing up in a cave.

How people left caves and learnt to make places like your home is the story of buildings. The way your house looks, whether it's old or new; the way it differs from the house next to it, from the church at the end of the road, the cathedral in your favourite city, the office where your parents work, the hospital you were born in and the school you study in – that's all part of the story too. And the story begins with people building houses to shelter them from the wind and rain, to protect their families from wild animals, and to keep their possessions safe from enemies.

As soon as people had invented better tools, they used them to build houses. People in forests built

Log cabin *Frame walls* *Diagonal braces* *Stone house*

cabins of logs. They cut down tall, straight trees, and made the walls by stacking one log on top of another. If they overlapped the logs at the corners, the walls were stronger. They found that sloping roofs were best for throwing off rain, but sloping roofs pushed the walls outwards, so they learnt how to link the walls with beams to hold them steady.

It's hard work cutting down trees, so before long people came up with easier ways to make houses from wood. They started with light frames for the walls, placing posts an arm's length apart with rails top and bottom, then covered the frames to keep the weather out. Sometimes they used overlapping planks as a covering, sometimes woven sticks that they plastered with mud or clay. They lined the frames on the inside as well, so their walls would be smooth and clean.

To make a good frame house, people had to invent strong ways to fit wood together. They also learnt that frames were less wobbly if they fitted them with diagonal pieces of wood to brace them.

Up in the mountains, people experimented with ways of sticking stones together. Some stones, if they were heated in an oven until they were incredibly

hot, gave off a white powder called lime. Although it burned their hands, people discovered that when they soaked lime in water and mixed it with sand, it made the kind of glue we call mortar. Using mortar, they were soon sticking stones together to build strong, high walls. They found their walls were even stronger when they overlapped square stones at the corners, just as forest dwellers did with the logs for their wooden cabins. Inside, they used the lime and sand mixture as plaster to smooth the stone walls.

People on seashores and in deserts even found a way to build shelters with mud. Rather than pile it in a heap, they turned it into bricks by packing it into wooden moulds and drying it in the sun. In the north, where the sun was cooler, they baked the bricks in ovens, or kilns, instead. Dried bricks could be used like little stones, and people quickly learnt the best ways of overlapping them to make their walls as strong as possible. People in deserts stopped their sun-baked bricks from cracking by plastering them on the outside with mud.

Whatever the walls of their houses were made of – wood, stone or brick – builders found the hardest thing of all was making a good roof. To begin with,

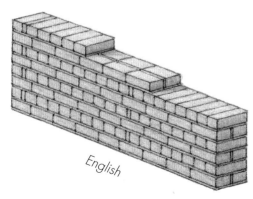

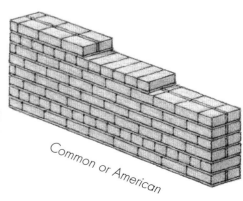

English *Flemish* *Common or American*

Different types of brickwork

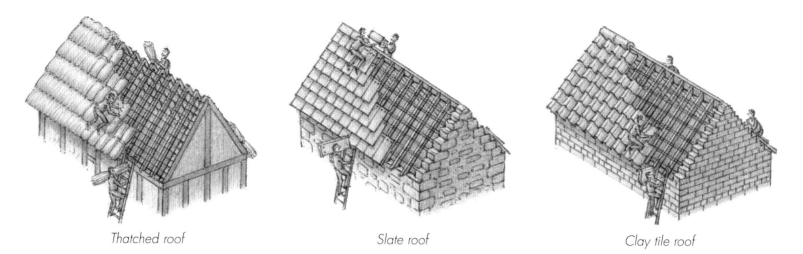

Thatched roof   *Slate roof*   *Clay tile roof*

they simply piled logs up in a roof shape, but however tightly they stuffed the cracks with grass and leaves, rain dripped through onto their beds. It was better, they found, to start by making their roofs as frames, using rafters. Then they could fix coverings over the rafters to keep out the rain. For the coverings, farmers gathered grass in bundles and tied it to the rafters as thatch. It made their houses look a bit shaggy but kept them dry inside. Mountain people covered their roofs in thin stones that they fixed onto the rafters in overlapping sheets. Slate made the best roofs because it could be split into sheets no thicker than their fingers. Builders who were moulding clay for bricks baked clay roof tiles as well, shaping them to help the rain run off faster.

The important thing for every kind of roof was to make it stick out over the walls to throw the rain as far from the house as possible.

And so, as the centuries went by, people learnt how to make log cabins, frame houses and stone huts, houses of brick, and houses of sun-baked mud or adobe. They experimented until their houses were strong enough to withstand the wind, and dry enough to keep out the rain. And wherever they lived, they built their houses in the way that suited them best. Some people were always on the move and needed houses they could pack up and carry with them. Native Americans, who travelled to follow the animals they hunted, carried tipis of sticks with leather hides stretched over them, while the Bedouin, whose flocks roamed for thousands of

miles, made tents they could load onto camels for the next day's journey. Fishermen built houses on stilts to raise them above floods. Mountain dwellers built overhanging roofs to throw off snow.

Houses looked different in different parts of the world because people built them from whatever materials they had to hand. Inuit hunters made shelters of packed snow that they called igloos. Fijians wove walls of reed. The Musgum of Cameroon built houses of earth and grass that looked like beehives. And because they were proud of their homes, people decorated them to make them special. Some scratched patterns in mud walls, while others painted their roofs in bright colours, or carved the faces of animals into the beams.

For thousands of years people built homes like these – as many people still do on every continent of the world. But all these houses had one big problem, however strong or beautiful they were.

They were all very uncomfortable.

To start with, they were dark. People cut square holes in the walls as windows, but windows let in the cold and rain, and when they closed them off with wooden shutters, their houses were as dark as ever. When night fell, there was nothing to light them with but smoky little oil lamps.

Next, they had no water, so there were no bathrooms or kitchens. People carried jars down to the stream, but the jars were heavy and it was hard not to spill the water on the way back. And when you needed

Stilt house

Inuit igloo

North American tipi

Ghanaian house with mud decorations

Bedouin tent

Musgum hut in Cameroon

Simple stone chimney

the toilet you had to go out in the rain and dig a hole in the ground.

Worst of all, houses were cold. At night, children lay shivering as icy draughts cut through cracks in the walls. Old people huddled under blankets but the cold still numbed them. When people tried lighting fires, their houses filled with smoke and everyone had to run outside coughing. It was better when they cut a hole in the roof to let the smoke out, but even so, fires were dangerous in houses of wood or thatch, and families would often return from the fields to find smoking ruins where their homes had once stood.

So in some parts of the world, as people grew richer, they invented ways to make their homes more comfortable.

They built chimneys so they could light fires indoors. Chimneys were made of brick or stone so they wouldn't burn, and took smoke safely out through the roof. After that, houses were much warmer, and people could cook indoors, rather than outside in the rain.

To make more space, people built upper floors from wooden beams covered with planks, and staircases so they could climb from one floor to another.

To make their homes brighter, they needed something

Staircase

that would let light in but keep rain out, so they used glass, which was made by heating sand and solidifying it in thin, hard sheets. Glass only came in small pieces to start with, but builders linked the pieces together with metal wire and fitted them in wooden frames to fill window openings. Thanks

to glass, people could sit indoors in bad weather and watch the rain drumming harmlessly against their windowpanes.

For centuries, glass was expensive so only the richest people could afford it. And it was the rich, of course, who made the most comfortable homes of all.

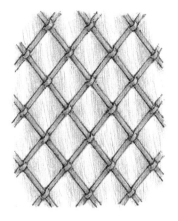

Early glass window

They plastered their walls smooth, then painted them with gorgeous decorations, or hung carpets and tapestries on them. They decorated their floors with precious stones, or mosaics – pictures made out of tiny stones fitted together. They had water brought to their houses in metal pipes so they didn't need to go to the well, and built sewers to take waste away. The Romans, who lived in Italy two thousand years ago, even invented central heating by raising their ground floors up on struts and blowing hot air under them.

Roman underfloor heating

And all the time, people kept finding new ways of building. The Romans made use of arches. Before then, no one could make really wide openings because beams were small and weak, but arches made of brick or stone were stronger than any beam and reached much further.

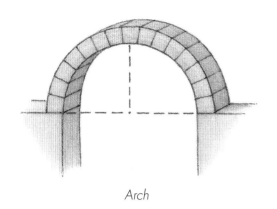

Arch

Bridge

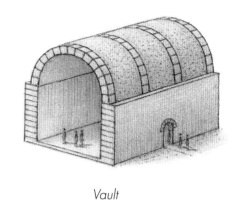

Vault

Using arches, people could build bridges firm enough to drive carts over, and wider openings for their windows. They even learnt to make long arches called vaults that covered whole rooms.

Next, the Romans invented concrete by mixing stone into the lime and sand they used for mortar. They poured the wet mixture into moulds and when it had dried, took the moulds away and found it set hard as stone. Concrete could be used to make foundations for walls, to lay flat floors and even to shape vaults.

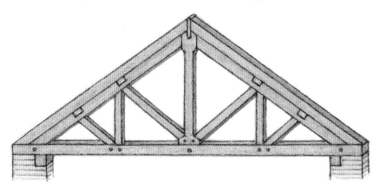

Wooden truss

Carpenters learnt to make small bits of wood cover wide spaces by fitting them together as trusses which, by balancing each piece of wood against the next, seemed to hang in the air by magic. In time they invented better ways to fix wood together to give their trusses strong, flexible joints.

By this time, many people lived in towns rather than farms or villages. The first towns formed around rivers or harbours, grew up where roads crossed to make a market-place, or appeared where soldiers camped around a king's palace. Because there was less space in towns, houses grew taller, rising four or five storeys into the air and teetering towards each other across narrow streets jammed with horses and carts. From their bedroom windows, town children stared at rooftops and blank walls instead of trees or hills. Gathering food didn't mean cutting it in the fields but going to the shop or marketplace. Water didn't come from clear streams; it was pumped in from the countryside through pipes. People who lived in towns and cities didn't build their own houses. Instead they rented apartments from landlords. In ancient Rome landlords built huge blocks of apartments called insulae or islands, where dozens of families crammed together around narrow courtyards, listening not to birdsong but to the sound of their neighbours quarrelling and traffic rumbling along the street outside.

Roman insula

Living in cities could be exciting but it was also dangerous. Families still cooked on open stoves, while bakers stoked their ovens to make bread, and smoke coiled into the air from a thousand hearths. Fires broke out all the time, and because the wooden houses were

The Great Fire of London

built so close together, it could leap quickly from house to house, alley to alley. The smell of burning would drift through open windows and people would hurry to gather their belongings and stampede downstairs. Often children were woken in the night to go outside and watch, shivering, while streets blazed and roofs collapsed in showers of sparks. To prevent fire spreading, cities passed laws to ban houses that rose too high or spread too far. After a great fire destroyed most of London, a law was passed that each house should be divided from the next by a brick wall.

Sometimes laws made buildings safer. Sometimes new inventions made them stronger. A merchant might come back from overseas with stories of a new way to hold up a roof or build a staircase, and everyone would copy it. At other times wars broke out, towns grew poor, and people forgot the skills their fathers had learnt. But still, for hundreds of years, people lived in homes of stone, brick or wood, roofed them with tiles, heated them with fires and lit them with oil lamps. It seemed as if they would live that way for ever.

And then, more than two hundred years ago, there was a change in the

Steel frame

way people made things. Chairs weren't made by craftsmen any more; they were made in factories, using machines. China plates were also made in factories; so were knives and forks, pots and pans; while carpet and cloth were woven by machines far more quickly than they could be made by hand. Today we call this change the Industrial Revolution, and it changed how buildings were made as well.

Inventors found new ways of making glass. Until then glass could be produced only in small panes, but they worked out how to make it in sheets so large and strong that builders could construct whole walls of it. They also discovered that several layers of glass fitted together, or double glazing, kept out the cold. Metal had been used in buildings for years to make locks and door hinges, or fix stones together, while lead, the softest of all metals, was used to fill gaps on roofs. But it wasn't strong enough to hold buildings up until inventors worked to improve two kinds of iron: cast iron and steel. A steel beam could reach much further than a wooden one and carry more weight. By bolting steel beams and columns together, engineers constructed vast frames that raised bigger buildings more quickly than ever before. They strengthened concrete as well, by pouring it around steel bars to make reinforced concrete.

With such strong new materials, buildings could become longer and wider.

Tudor houses

Georgian terrace

There was no point making them taller, though, because people got tired climbing too many stairs. But when an American, Elisha Otis, invented an elevator that took people from floor to floor automatically, there was no limit to the height of buildings, and towers soared into the sky.

Otis's elevator worked on electricity, which completely changed how people lived. In the past, houses were lit only by oil lamps and candles which gave out such a dim glow that most people went to bed at sunset and rose at dawn to make the most of the sun's light. Gas lamps, which were invented soon after the Industrial Revolution, burned better than candles, but electric lights shone brighter still. They lit homes so brilliantly that people could stay up all night, reading, talking or eating. In towns that had once been dark after sundown, every window glowed and chains of street lamps shone on the cobbles.

New inventions made houses warmer as well as brighter. Gas boilers heated water and pumped it through radiators to heat homes without the smell and

Parisian apartments

danger of an open fire. In the past, everyone had to fetch their water from streams – as many people in the world still do today. But in richer countries, pipes were laid to bring water, both hot and cold, to bathrooms and kitchens in every home. People simply had to turn a tap to get as much water as they liked.

If you look at the home you live in, you can see how far people have come since living in caves. You can probably see how your house was built – whether it's a frame or has brick walls; whether it's made of wood or concrete. You might even be able to guess when it was built. If it's made of rough stone, or crooked timbers filled in with plaster, it's probably very old. In the eighteenth century houses in some countries were built as "terraces" – side by side, with windows only at the front and back. Older terraces were mostly finished in brick, while later they were plastered and painted. If your home is in the middle of a city, it's probably in an apartment block where everyone shares the hallway and stairs. If it's a twentieth-century building, it might be a tower block, soaring high into the air.

Modern high-rise

But homes, of course, are not the only kind of buildings. Look out of your window and you'll see shops and offices, factories and schools, police stations, hospitals and warehouses. From the moment people learnt to raise walls and cover roofs, they used their skills to make shelters for many different reasons. Farmers put up sheds for their animals, coops for their chickens, and barns to store the crops they grew. Carpenters built workshops. Blacksmiths built forges where sparks flew from their hammers. Merchants built warehouses

Barns

to store the cloth and spices, wine and oil they brought back from overseas. In towns, people built shops and markets, pubs and meeting halls; they built law courts where criminals were tried, hospitals where sick people could be cured and schools for children to learn in. To give themselves somewhere to relax after work, they built theatres, circuses, sports grounds and racetracks.

Harbour

Windmill

People used stone, brick and wood for other purposes too. Engineers constructed wharves to build ships in and harbours to dock them. They bridged rivers, dammed lakes, and cut tunnels through mountains. They built windmills on hilltops to catch energy from the wind, and watermills whose wheels were turned by streams rushing along valleys. When wars broke out, kings built castles protected with ramparts and battlements, and ringed their towns with strong walls.

Since the Industrial Revolution, every new invention has needed new buildings to serve it. Electricity

Watermill

needed power stations to generate it. Machines needed factories whose chimneys belched smoke into the sky, and whose clatter echoed from the hills. When railways began to link town to town, engineers invented railway stations. As aeroplanes developed, they laid out runways and airports. People keep inventing things, and they'll keep inventing new kinds of buildings too – buildings we haven't seen yet, to do things we can't even imagine.

Some buildings were always designed with special care. Kings wanted their palaces to show people how powerful they were, so they built great halls for their followers to gather in and throne rooms where they could deliver orders. Worshippers wanted the places

Railway station

others what they care about and what they believe in. So they make them as beautiful as possible – or sometimes, if they're making a fortress or prison, as scary as possible. And that's why buildings change the way we feel. They can fill us with awe or calm, joy or dread. They can be so lovely they make us never want to leave; so cruel and ugly that we hurry out of the door determined never to go back.

Factory

they prayed in to show how much they honoured God. Muslims decorated their mosques with rich tiles, Hindus carved stone into intricate patterns, Christians raised churches on soaring columns, and Jews filled their synagogues with candles. People don't only build buildings to serve a purpose. They want them to show

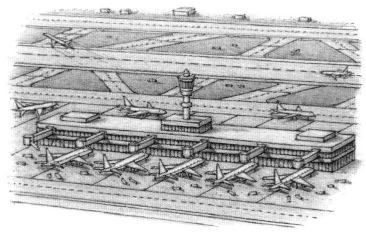

Airport

Buildings are far more than piles of brick or frames of steel, because every one, no matter how large or small, carries the dreams of the people who made it. You can't look at a building without wondering who lives or works there. You can't visit a building without asking yourself who built it and why. And as you stare at buildings and wonder about the people inside them, you understand that that's what makes them so special.

Every building has a story to tell.

Power station

THE KING WHO CONQUERED TIME
The Pyramid of Djoser, Saqqara, Egypt, 2650 BCE

Deep in the heart of Africa, the great River Nile rises from underground and begins its journey north to the sea. Along the way its water brings life to the fields around it, making seeds sprout and plants grow. Long, long ago, farmers gathered to till and plant their crops along the riverbank, and that was how the land of Egypt was born.

The Egyptians used the river to travel as well as water their crops. They sailed the Nile in boats of reed, trading and spreading news. Egypt became rich and well organized, a country not only of farmers but of merchants and sailors. Its ruler was a mighty king known as the pharaoh.

Farmers live among the fields they work in, but merchants gather in towns. The first towns were built by the rivers Tigris and Euphrates, to the north-east of Egypt. The pharaohs heard stories of life in those towns: of vast brick temples raised on platforms that

could be seen for miles, of powerful armies, of mighty leaders whose palaces were decorated with carved animals. So they built temples and palaces of their own, raised their own armies and set out to conquer their neighbours.

The greatest of all Egypt's rulers was Pharaoh Djoser. He extended his kingdom far into Africa and Arabia, and his people worshipped him as a god. But as time went by an uneasy feeling began to keep Djoser awake at night, plucking the sheets and staring for hours into the darkness. He was the most powerful man in the world but one day he would die just like the poorest beggar. He had defeated all his enemies but he could never conquer time.

His priests tried to reassure him. They told him that after he died he would live among the gods. It made no difference to the pharaoh. His body would still crumble to dust. His family would die; his servants would die;

other kings would conquer Egypt. In a thousand, five thousand, years, who would know the name of Djoser?

One night he walked out into the desert. The moon shone on the sand dunes. In the distance he could see mountains. And a thought came to him. Mountains didn't die. Rock didn't crumble to dust. A man lives only one short lifetime but rock lasts for ever. So what if he built himself a tomb of rock? Surely his name would last for ever!

The next morning, Djoser ordered his minister, Imhotep, to build a tomb of stone. It would be the most magnificent Egypt had ever seen. Pharaohs of the past had raised square mounds of earth and brick as tombs, but the desert wind soon scoured away their walls. A stone tomb would defy the sandstorms. It would defy time itself.

Imhotep trained his masons to smooth the face of the stone and set it in blocks to make a single, flat wall. When they had raised a square mound for the base

of the tomb, Imhotep ordered them to build a smaller square on top of it, and another on top of that; and so on until a vast, white pyramid of stone – a man-made mountain – towered against the blue Egyptian sky.

Next he planned a shrine to stand alongside the pyramid. Most shrines didn't last long, for their brick walls cracked in the sun and their wooden columns rotted. But Imhotep ordered everything to be made of stone.

The walls of the shrine were as smooth as the pyramid and decorated with carved grooves that cast shadows when the sun fell on them. The entrance was placed at the very centre, and other openings balanced equally to either side. Inside, Imhotep ordered his men to build great columns of stone to hold up the roof. Wooden columns were usually decorated with bundles of reeds, so the masons carved their stone columns to look like reed bundles as well. The tops, or capitals, of wooden columns were decorated with palm leaves, so they carved stone capitals that swelled out like the leaves of the palm tree. Imhotep summoned the best artists in Egypt to decorate the walls, and the shrine rang to the sound of hammers as Djoser's great monument filled with pictures describing his battles and conquests.

When Djoser died, musicians played as his body was laid in the pyramid and the door sealed. Other pharaohs followed him and built pyramids of their own. For thousands of years the kingdom of Egypt endured; but at last, just as Djoser had feared, it was conquered by other, more powerful, kingdoms, and the pharaohs were overthrown.

Djoser's great pyramid at Saqqara didn't fall, though. It remained like a mountain against the Egyptian sky. Sandstorms buried his shrine. But when it was dug out, thousands of years later, its walls were as smooth and strong as ever.

Today, people still travel to Egypt to marvel at the pharaohs' power and wealth. Djoser was right: kings may die, but stone lasts for ever.

PYRAMID OF DJOSER

The tomb Imhotep built for Pharaoh Djoser wasn't a single building, but a vast complex of rooms, corridors and courtyards with the pyramid at the centre.

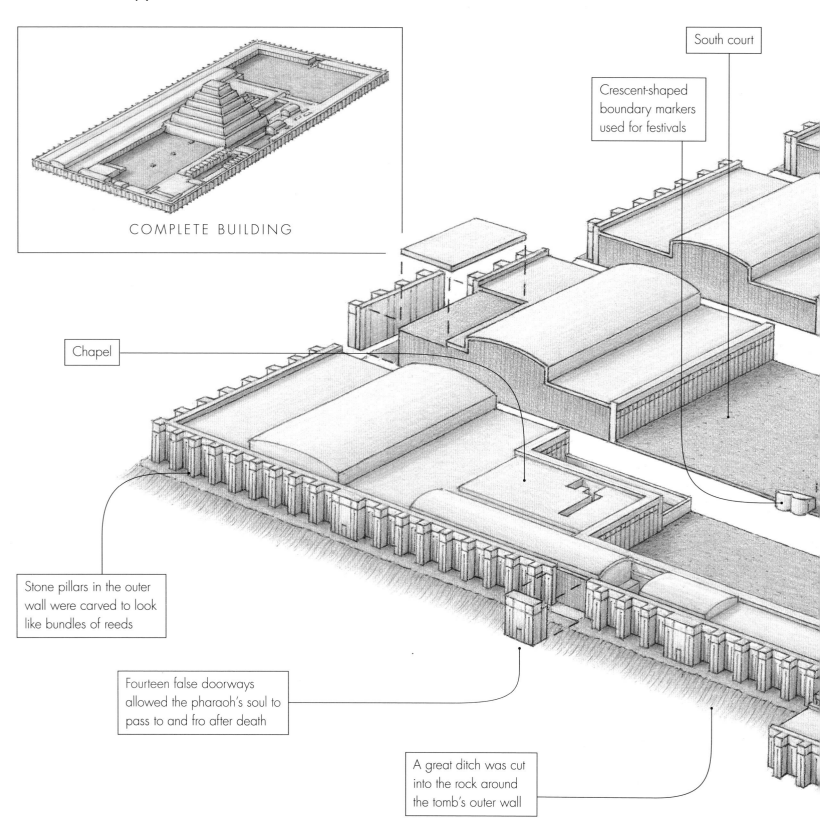

COMPLETE BUILDING

South court

Crescent-shaped boundary markers used for festivals

Chapel

Stone pillars in the outer wall were carved to look like bundles of reeds

Fourteen false doorways allowed the pharaoh's soul to pass to and fro after death

A great ditch was cut into the rock around the tomb's outer wall

PYRAMIDS AND TEMPLES

The pharaohs ruled Egypt for thousands of years. Many copied Djoser and built tombs. At Giza the pharaohs Cheops, Chephren and Mycerinus raised three vast pyramids clad in shining stone. They can still be seen outside Cairo today.

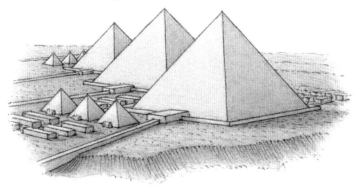

The great pyramids at Giza

The pharaohs built shrines to their gods as well. At Thebes, their capital, they raised temples to gods like Amon and Khons. To fill visitors with awe, the avenues leading to the temples were lined with carved monsters, each temple was approached through a courtyard ringed with columns, and the entrance door was set in a vast wall of stone. Inside, the temples were dark because the Egyptians didn't know how to cover rooms with vaults or trusses, so they had to set columns close together. Visitors stumbled through the shadows with the columns towering over them like the trunks of stone trees in a forest of rock.

Temple at Luxor

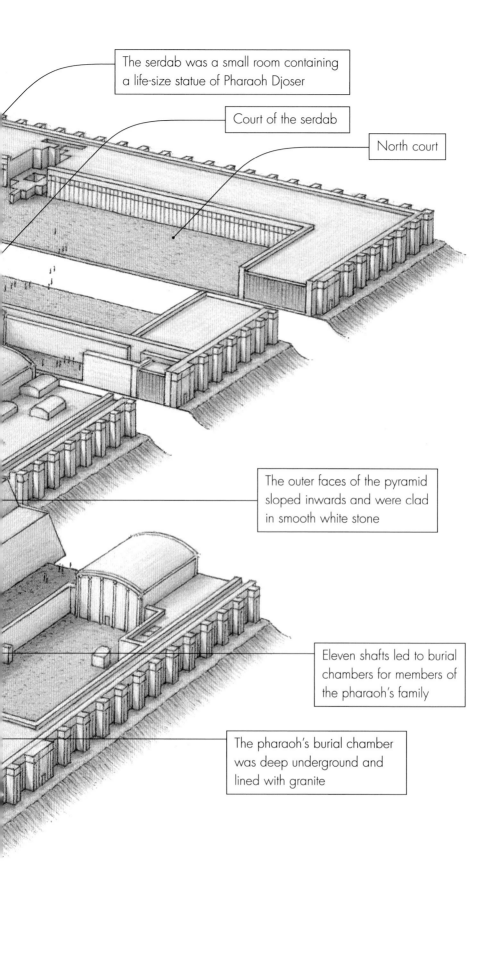

The serdab was a small room containing a life-size statue of Pharaoh Djoser

Court of the serdab

North court

The outer faces of the pyramid sloped inwards and were clad in smooth white stone

Eleven shafts led to burial chambers for members of the pharaoh's family

The pharaoh's burial chamber was deep underground and lined with granite

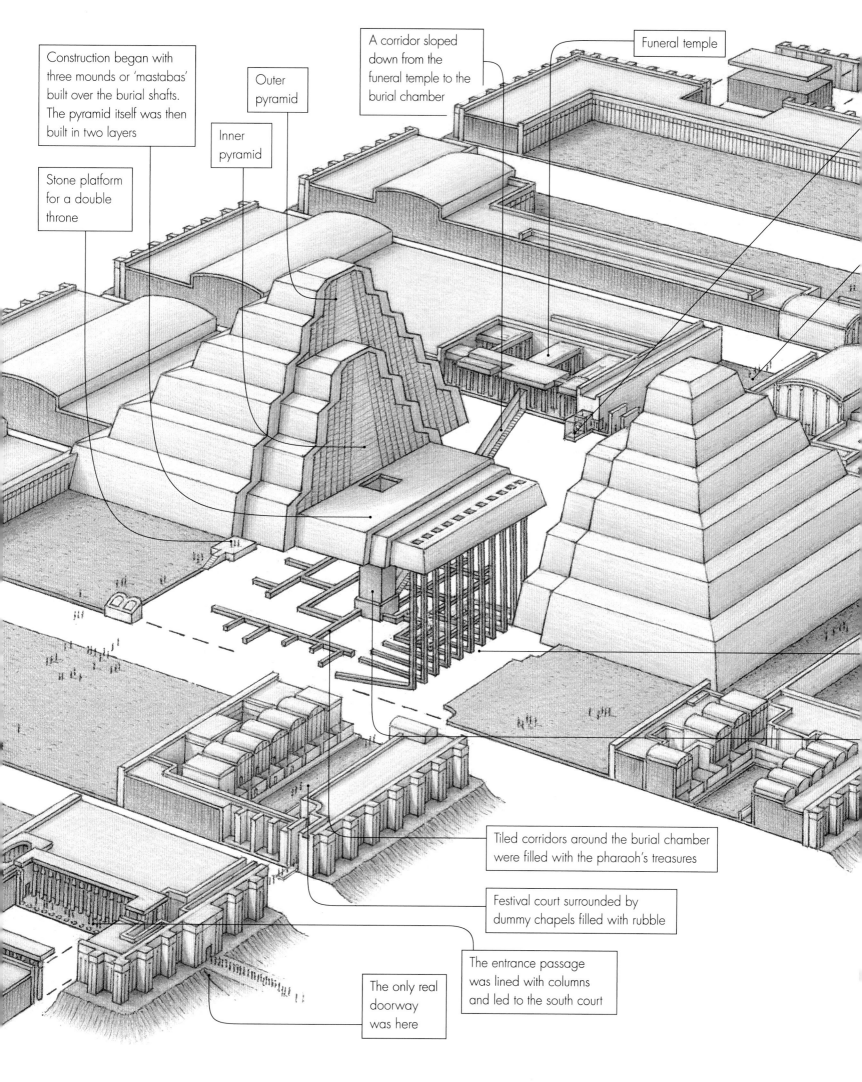

Construction began with three mounds or 'mastabas' built over the burial shafts. The pyramid itself was then built in two layers

Outer pyramid

Inner pyramid

A corridor sloped down from the funeral temple to the burial chamber

Funeral temple

Stone platform for a double throne

Tiled corridors around the burial chamber were filled with the pharaoh's treasures

Festival court surrounded by dummy chapels filled with rubble

The only real doorway was here

The entrance passage was lined with columns and led to the south court

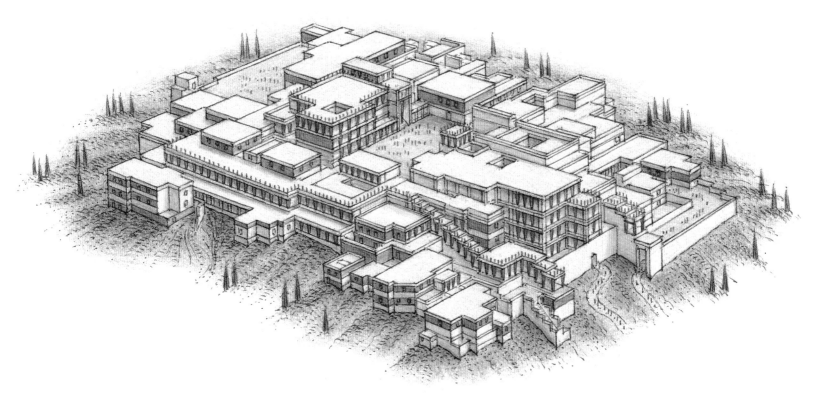

The palace complex at Knossos, Crete

THE TEMPLES OF GREECE

From the Pyramid of Djoser to the Parthenon

The River Nile flows into the Mediterranean Sea, so the Egyptians began to trade with the people who lived on the islands of Greece. Greek merchants brought back wonderful stories of the pharaohs' temples and palaces, and Greek kings began to build palaces in the same way.

The people of Greece, who were farmers and fishermen, had never seen such buildings. The palace of King Minos at Knossos, in Crete, was so big people called it a labyrinth and joked that visitors got lost wandering from room to room. They made up stories of a monster at the heart of the palace that would eat anyone who lost their way. One story was about a prince called Theseus who was brought from Athens to be thrown to the monster. Ariadne, Minos's daughter, fell in love with Theseus and gave him a ball of thread to unwind as he went into the labyrinth. In the story Theseus killed the monster, felt his way back along the thread and ran away with Ariadne.

The Greeks loved to tell each other such stories as they sat at night in the halls of their palaces. But bad

Early Greek stone temple

times came to Greece. An earthquake toppled Minos's labyrinth. Wars started, armies invaded and the other palaces were burnt. Gradually their ruins disappeared. Creepers wound round beams and thrust through walls. Roofs collapsed and earth built up over them, burying the great halls where stories had been told, the hearths where fires had burned and the beautiful paintings which had once covered the walls. The palaces were forgotten.

Hundreds of years later, archaeologists went searching for them. They asked Greek farmers if there was any sign of ancient ruins nearby and would sometimes hear that in a particular field, ploughs often caught on fragments of pottery, or a certain hill was full of old bronze arrowheads. Often they found nothing. But sometimes, as they dug deep underground, their trowels rang on stone, and they would find the edge of a wall or the face of a broken statue. Then, carefully sweeping aside the soil, they would uncover walls and floors, decorated jars that no one had drunk from for centuries, or paintings of dolphins that no eye had seen since the day the palace fell.

After the palaces were ruined, long centuries passed before peace returned to Greece and people began to think of building again. They started by raising temples to the gods they worshipped: to Zeus, king of the gods, and Hera, his queen; to Apollo, the sun god; and to Athena, the goddess of wisdom. They built in wood, surrounding their temples with columns and giving them sloping roofs to throw the rain off. Gradually,

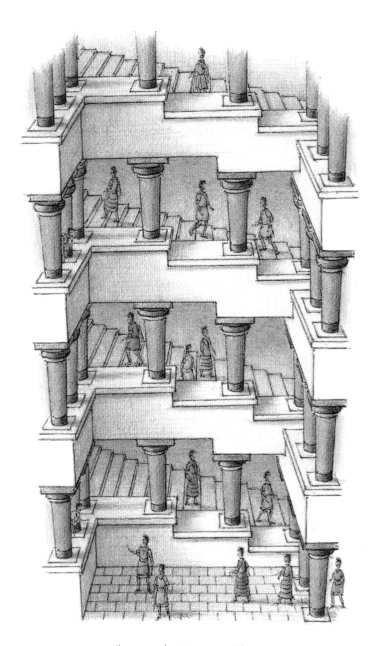

The grand staircase at Knossos

Early Greek wooden temple

as their cities became wealthier, the Greeks started to build temples in stone, cutting it from the mountains that towered around them. They carved patterns in the stone and decorated them in vivid red, blue and gold paint. They filled the gable ends of the roofs, or pediments, with statues of gods and heroes.

Every town competed to make the most magnificent temple, but it was Athens that built the finest of all. It was called the Parthenon, and is still famous for its beauty today. But it arose from a catastrophe that nearly destroyed the city.

THE PEOPLE'S PROCESSION

The Parthenon, Athens, Greece, 447 BCE

High over the roofs of Athens, its cliffs rising sheer above the streets and markets, stands a rock called the Acropolis. In ancient times it was the stronghold of the city. The Athenians retreated there in times of danger, they gathered there in times of triumph, and they covered the hill's crest with fine temples. The finest of all was dedicated to the city's patron, Athena Parthenos, goddess of wisdom. The roof of the Parthenon could be seen from the mountains around the city, and even from ships out at sea, where passing sailors marvelled at the wealth of Athens.

Every four years the citizens of Athens marched up to the Acropolis in procession to put a new robe on the great statue of Athena that stood there. The procession showed what was special about Athens. For there was no king riding at the head of the people. Long before, the citizens had got rid of their kings and begun to rule themselves. Instead of obeying a king's orders they gathered in assemblies to argue, debate and vote on what to do.

The Athenians prospered in their free town, but one day a shadow fell over their freedom. Far to the east, where the sun rose each morning, lay the mighty empire of the Persians. To the towns close by, the Athenians seemed powerful and rich, but they were feeble compared with Persia's Great King, whose armies conquered the pharaohs of Egypt, spread his empire for thousands of miles, and swallowed up any country who defied them. When the Great King Darius quarrelled with the Greeks, he sent his armies to devour the little towns of Greece as well.

The Athenians gathered in their assembly and voted to fight back. They knew they were outnumbered, but there was no time for the other Greeks to send help. Each citizen sharpened his sword. Each free man buckled on his armour. Grimly they marched north and, at the Battle of Marathon, defeated the Great King's army. That night the Athenians lit fires outside the Parthenon to celebrate.

But their triumph didn't last long. Soon afterwards Darius died, but his son Xerxes vowed to take revenge on the Greeks who had defied his father. He gathered a new army whose ranks swarmed into Greece, and launched a navy whose ships covered the horizon with sails. This time the Greeks seemed to have no chance. Some Spartans made a brave stand at the pass of Thermopylae, but Xerxes' army swept them aside, burst through the walls of Athens and set the city on fire.

By then the Athenians had taken to their ships. From far away they watched black smoke coil up from the Acropolis as the Parthenon burned.

The sea was their last refuge. And on it they determined to fight. When the Persian navy swept into the bay, the Athenians were ready for them. The battle that followed turned the sea the colour of blood and raged all day until the waves were covered with the wreckage of Persian ships. Only as night fell did the Athenians know they had won.

Xerxes' army marched home, but the Athenians returned to a city in ruins. Houses were burnt and shops ravaged, while nothing remained of the temples on the Acropolis but blackened timbers and scorched marble.

Pericles, the Athenians' leader, encouraged them to rebuild their city, but it took many years to repair public buildings and markets, and build houses for all the people who had lost their homes. All that time the ruins of the Parthenon stood forlorn on the Acropolis. Pericles often climbed up there to look down on the city he loved. From among the heaps of charred stone, he could see politicians arguing in the assembly, audiences cheering in the theatre and philosophers debating in the marketplace. That was what made Athens special, he thought. Athenians had used their wealth not to build tombs or palaces for kings, but on better things: on thinking, talking, wondering. It wasn't for nothing that the city was named after the goddess of wisdom.

The Persians didn't just want to ruin our monuments, he thought. They wanted to destroy our whole way of life.

And when, at last, the Athenians had time and money to rebuild their temple, Pericles was determined the new Parthenon would show everyone what the city stood for. It must be perfectly proportioned, perfectly decorated. It must be a temple to Athens itself.

He ordered great blocks of marble to be carted all the way from Mount Pentelicon. He hired Phidias, Greece's most famous sculptor, to plan the building and carve the decorations. Phidias put all his skill into the plans. He decided to give the temple eight columns across the front,

instead of the usual six. He laboured over the temple's height and width so that they would seem exactly balanced. He checked the proportions of even the finest detail: the rise of the steps and pitch of the roof, the height of the stonework in comparison to the columns, the width of the columns, how much they tapered, and the exact space between them.

From a distance, buildings often seem to bulge out slightly, so Phidias made the Parthenon's sides curve in. Columns often look as if they're leaning outwards, so he made them slope in just enough to look right. From whichever direction people saw it, from the mountains around Athens or from ships far out at sea, the new Parthenon would crown the Acropolis, stone glowing in the sunshine, as if it had stood there for ever.

Phidias decorated the temple with some of the greatest carvings he had ever made. On one pediment he told the story of Athena's birth; the other showed how the Athenians had chosen her as their goddess. Above the columns he carved centaurs, half-man, half-horse, battling with gods. But the finest carving of all was the frieze – a sort of carved strip cartoon – that stretched around the inside of the colonnade.

For that, Phidias chose as his subject the procession of the citizens of Athens when they marched up to the Acropolis together to give their statue of Athena a new robe. His workshop filled with the tap of hammers as he and his stonemasons carved magistrates in their gowns and horses stamping in the morning air. They carved girls waiting in line and young men flicking the reins of their chariots. They carved beasts snorting, women waiting patiently, and priests carrying gifts for the goddess in their arms. Every Athenian knew and loved those procession mornings: the chilly dawn air spiced with the smell of incense, the children being hushed by their parents and the solemn faces of the elders. Now they were captured in stone for ever. And Pericles, who visited the building every day, gazed up at the frieze with pride.

The Parthenon was more than a temple to a goddess. The Athenians were part of it themselves.

THE PARTHENON

The Parthenon was a Doric temple (see side flap) with eight columns under each pediment and seventeen along the sides. Inside were two rooms. One contained a statue of Athena. The other was used as a treasury.

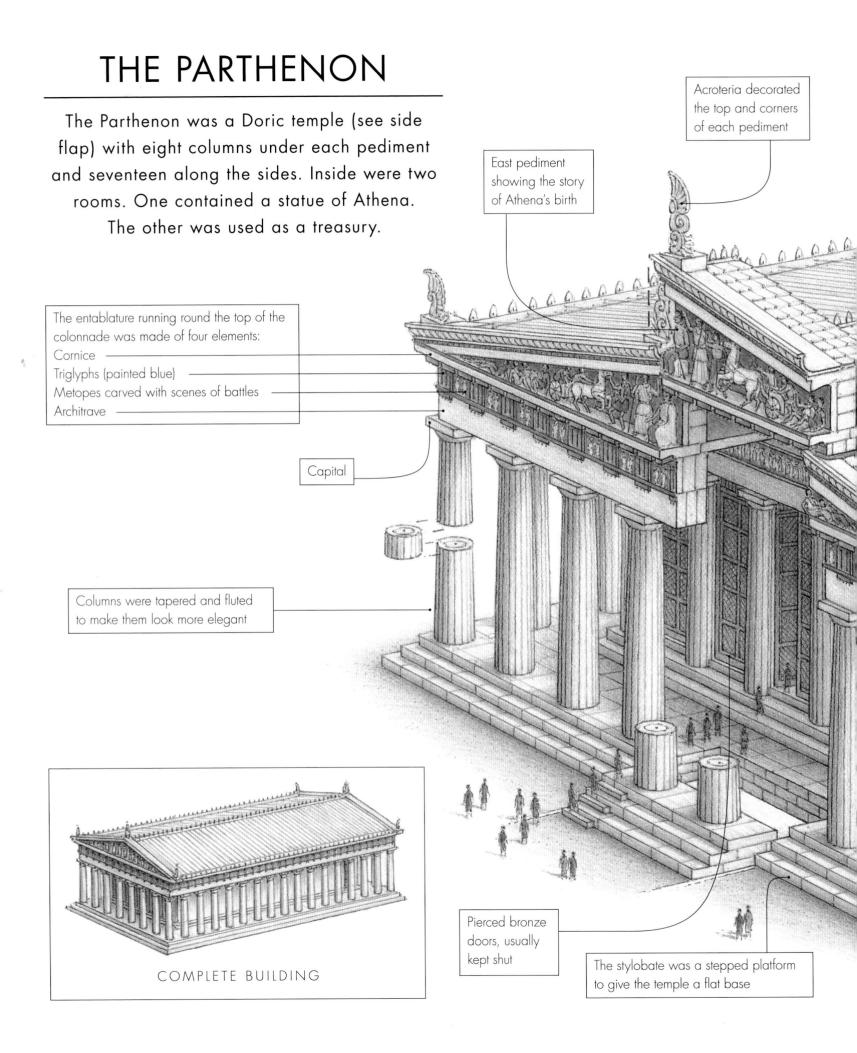

Acroteria decorated the top and corners of each pediment

East pediment showing the story of Athena's birth

The entablature running round the top of the colonnade was made of four elements:
Cornice
Triglyphs (painted blue)
Metopes carved with scenes of battles
Architrave

Capital

Columns were tapered and fluted to make them look more elegant

Pierced bronze doors, usually kept shut

The stylobate was a stepped platform to give the temple a flat base

COMPLETE BUILDING

THE CLASSICAL ORDERS

The Greeks invented sets of rules, or orders, for how stone temples should look. The buildings made by the Greeks and Romans using the orders of architecture are known as classical.

Doric columns were short, ribbed or fluted on the sides, and sloped inwards towards the top. They held up a carved stone beam that was decorated with stone blocks to look like the beams of wooden temples.

Ionic columns were slimmer than Doric and curved gracefully from bottom to top. The capitals at the tops of Ionic columns were decorated with scrolls that looked like rams' horns.

The third order was Corinthian. Corinthian columns were the most elaborate of all. Their capitals were decorated to look like the frilly leaves of the acanthus plant.

Later the Romans came up with another version of the Doric order; and a fifth order, the simplest of all, known as Tuscan.

The classical orders were set out using mathematical proportions. For example, Doric and Tuscan columns were usually seven or eight times as high as their width, Ionic columns were nine times as high, and Corinthian nine and a half times.

as Athens'
of silver

Marble
roof tiles

Wooden
rafters

The forty-six Doric
columns of the outer
colonnade were
made in segments

Walls made
of stone
blocks fixed
with metal
cramps

Musicians

Men carrying
holy water for
the ceremony

Cows and
sheep to be
sacrificed in
the ceremony

C PROCESSION visited the temple every four years. It was the same procession
the carved frieze, 160m long by 1m high, that ran round the Parthenon's colonnade

The main room in the Parthenon, the naos, contained a giant statue of Athena

Two-storey colonnade around the statue

The gold and ivory statue of Athena, made by Phidias, was so big that the statue in its right hand was as tall as a person

Ionic columns in the treasury

Inner room use treasury. Ches were stored he

The leader of the procession carried a new robe for Athena's statue

Priestesses of Athena

The pool of water in front of the statue reflected light onto it and stopped the ivory drying out

Women bearing gifts

THE PANATHENA
Phidias depicted or

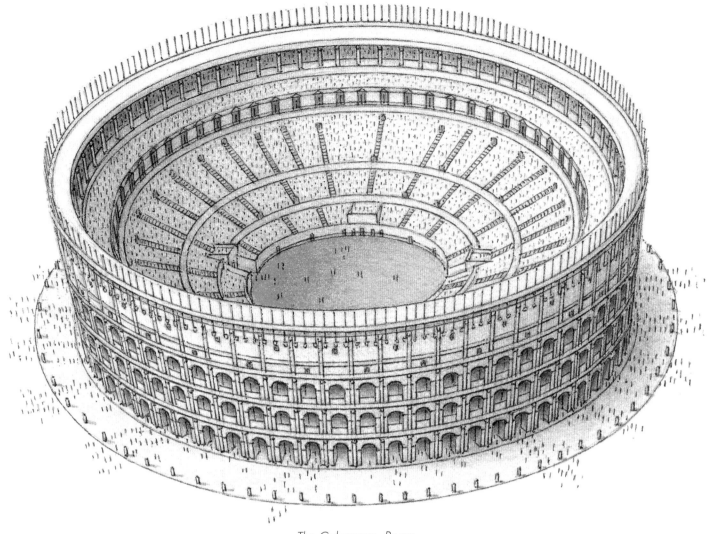

The Colosseum, Rome

THE ROMANS

From the Parthenon to Hagia Sophia

Greek travellers built temples wherever they settled, and all over the Mediterranean people copied them. When the city of Rome in Italy grew rich, its citizens covered their hills with buildings in the Greek style, and as they conquered their neighbours and turned Rome into a mighty empire, they built monuments wherever they went. From Africa to Scotland, Spain to Asia, classical buildings rose above towns decorated with columns and enriched with statues.

The Roman army employed engineers who were skilled at setting out camps, building roads and bridging rivers. In the provinces the Romans founded, their engineers laid out new towns like Londinium (London), with law courts for the magistrates, wharves for the merchants, and aqueducts to bring fresh water from the countryside. Roman engineers were always looking for new ways to build. Because there was no stone in many of the places they conquered, they became skilful at building with bricks. They learnt how to make arches so that they could span rooms wider than ever before. For the circuses Romans loved so much they raised tiers of arches in a ring around the stage. They made brick walls higher and stronger by filling them with a mixture of rubble and mortar. And that was how they discovered a whole new material: concrete.

Lime is a kind of glue made by burning limestone

in a kiln. Mix it with sand and you have mortar to hold bricks together. Mix stones in with the mortar and you have concrete. Concrete is cheap and strong. Best of all, if you pour it into moulds while it is still wet, it can be made into any shape you like.

To start with, the Romans used concrete for foundations and walls, but they soon found it could be poured into the shape of a tunnel to make a vault. Most buildings were still narrow inside, because their roofs were no wider than the wooden beams supporting them – even the Parthenon was dark and cramped inside. Using vaults, engineers could make rooms far bigger and grander. And then they came up with an even better idea. They took an arch and spun it round in a circle. It made a shape like a ball cut in half: a dome. When you stood under it, the roof curved over your head like the sky itself.

In Rome the Emperor Hadrian decided to rebuild the Pantheon, a temple to all the gods, and ordered his architects to cover it with a vast dome of concrete.

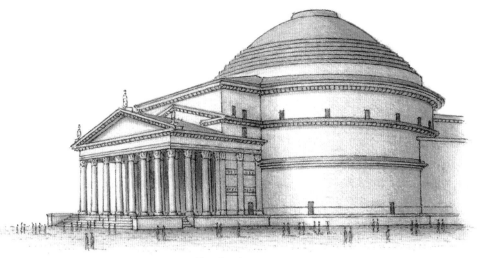

The Pantheon

No one was sure whether it could be done or not. For months workmen laboured over the wooden scaffolding that would support the dome while the concrete set, and engineers built models and checked calculations. They decided to make the concrete as thin as possible so it wouldn't be too heavy, and to leave a hole at the top to let light in. Then they mixed lime, sand and rubble, poured it in and waited.

Most people said it was impossible to roof so large a space. Everyone worried the walls wouldn't be strong enough. Nervously the engineers climbed the scaffold each morning to see if the concrete was set. And at last they gave orders for the scaffold to be removed.

Only now would they find out whether their idea had worked, or whether the dome of the Pantheon would crash to the ground and crush them all. They held their breath as the workmen knocked away the last strut. And then cheers echoed around the new temple – the dome had worked. There, soaring above them, was a great arching curve with a blinding disc of sunlight in the centre. Going into the Pantheon felt like diving into the sea. The dome soared overhead; light poured down from above, cascading off every ledge and recess and setting the marble walls on fire. Domes made a completely new kind of room. For the first time, buildings weren't grand just because of their grand decorations. It was the space inside them that made them beautiful.

And it was in another city, far east of Rome, that the Romans built the greatest dome of all, in the Church of Hagia Sophia, in Constantinople.

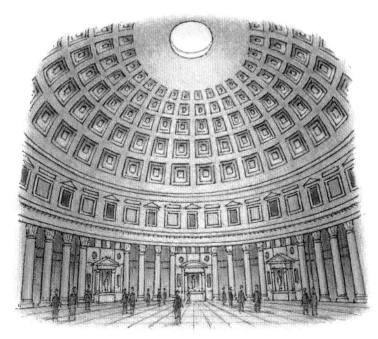

The interior of the Pantheon

THE HEART OF THE CITY

Hagia Sophia, Istanbul, Turkey, 532

Over time, the Roman Empire grew so big that one emperor couldn't govern it all, so the Emperor Diocletian divided it into two halves. The western half was ruled from Rome. The east lacked a capital city until the Emperor Constantine laid out a great town on the banks of the Bosphorus – the sea dividing Europe from Asia – and named it after himself: Constantinople.

Constantine was determined that his new city would be as great as Rome itself, so he filled it with statues, gardens and colonnades, and laid out stadiums, circuses, law courts and baths. But Constantinople was a city with a difference, for unlike the emperors who came before him, Constantine didn't believe in the old gods whose temples filled Rome. He was a Christian and wanted the greatest building in his city to be a church. He dedicated it to Holy Wisdom – Hagia Sophia in Greek.

After Constantine's death, Constantinople became more and more magnificent. His church of Hagia Sophia was replaced with a larger one, and when that was destroyed in a fire, the Emperor Justinian set out to enlarge it again. He sent for two of the most famous scientists in Europe, Isidore of Miletus and Anthemius of Tralles, and his order to them was simple. He had read in the Bible about the great temple King Solomon had built for the Jews in Jerusalem. He wanted Hagia Sophia to be greater still.

Isidore and Anthemius planned a church where arch would rise from arch, vault from vault, to a central dome that soared high above the city. They imagined light pouring from a thousand windows like water tumbling from the mouths of a fountain. Isidore was a scientist and Anthemius a mathematician. They worked out how to carry the weight of each vault onto a stone support or buttress, and how to set each arch springing from the last. When the whole space was roofed, they sent in craftsmen skilled in paintings and mosaics to cover the walls with gilded decoration.

"*Solomon,*" muttered Justinian when he visited the new church, "*I have surpassed you!*"*

The people of Constantinople gasped when they

*Quotations in italics are from historical sources.

of Byzantium, looked down from the walls and knew his city could hold out no longer. The armies of the Ottoman Sultan Mehmet II spread as far as the horizon. His ships filled the sea.

Constantine walked slowly through the streets to the Church of Hagia Sophia. Inside, priests chanted, candles flared, and smoke wreathed upwards towards the dome, just as it had for nearly a thousand years. How often had Byzantines come here to worship when danger threatened their walls? How many prayers had echoed from the dome? Now men and women crowded round its altars, desperately praying for God's help. If Hagia Sophia was Byzantium's heart, it was now throbbing pitifully at the city's death. Constantine lit a candle and prayed with the others, but he knew there was no escape for the city. Tomorrow Hagia Sophia would be in the hands of the Ottomans.

At dawn Mehmet's soldiers burst through the walls. They raced from street to street, setting fire to houses and slaughtering the defenders. When they reached the great church, they battered down the doors, chased out the priests and began tearing the gold mosaics from the walls. One by one the candles on the great altar were put out. The Christian prayers of Hagia Sophia came to an end for ever.

But when Mehmet himself arrived soon afterwards, he felt no wish to destroy the great church. The Ottomans were Muslim, and the Muslims had built many beautiful mosques, like the Mosque of Uqba at Kairouan and the Mosque of Ibn Tulun in Cairo. Hagia Sophia, Mehmet thought, could be the most beautiful of them all. So he ordered the church to be converted. Though the prayers of the Christians were silenced, Hagia Sophia became a mosque, and the Muslim *shahada* sounded from its vault.

Byzantium – or Istanbul, as it is now known – became the capital of the Ottoman Empire, but Hagia Sophia still soars above the Bosphorus and, 1500 years after it was built, its dome still hovers in the air "*as though it were suspended from heaven by a golden chain*".

first entered Hagia Sophia. The topmost dome hung in the air "*as though it were suspended from heaven by a golden chain*". Isidore and Anthemius seemed to have made a building not of brick or stone, but of space and light.

The church became the heart of Constantine's city. It wasn't just the centre of Constantinople – or Byzantium, as most people called it. It was the place Byzantines dreamt of when they were abroad. As they neared home, sailors crowded their ship's bows, watching for its dome to rise above the horizon like the peak of a mountain. Emperors were crowned under the mosaics of Hagia Sophia; emperors were buried beneath its marble floor. For nearly a thousand years priests chanted, candles winked on its golden walls and incense floated up to its mighty dome. Great buildings aren't just beautiful works of art; they carry people's dreams and hopes. Hagia Sophia carried the dreams of a whole empire.

Gradually, though, that empire grew weaker. Soldiers from the west attacked Byzantium, burnt palaces and stole statues. From what is now Turkey, in the east, a new power, the Ottoman Empire, appeared, and its forces drew closer with each year that passed. At last the day came when Constantine XI, the last emperor

HAGIA SOPHIA

The Parthenon was more beautiful on the outside than the inside. Hagia Sophia was the other way round. It was the interior, with its dome, its windows and mosaics, that took every visitor's breath away.

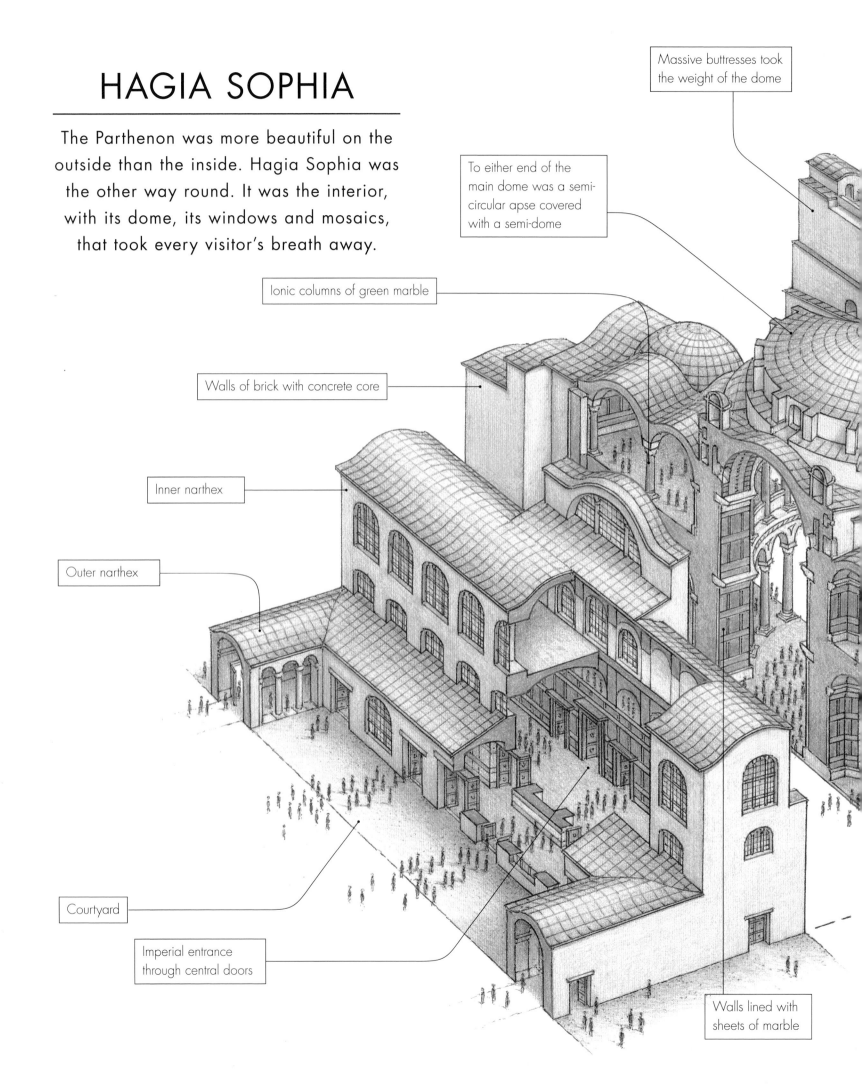

Massive buttresses took the weight of the dome

To either end of the main dome was a semi-circular apse covered with a semi-dome

Ionic columns of green marble

Walls of brick with concrete core

Inner narthex

Outer narthex

Courtyard

Imperial entrance through central doors

Walls lined with sheets of marble

ARCHES AND DOMES

Arches push outwards onto the walls they stand on. To stop the walls from falling, engineers strengthen them with buttresses that push back in. Domes are the same. They push outwards in every direction, as if they actually want to shove the walls away and tumble to the ground.

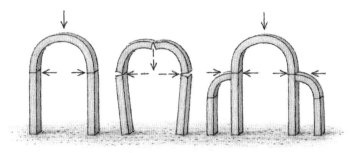

Arches and buttresses

So the engineers of Hagia Sophia, Isidore and Anthemius, set half-domes against the walls to push back. The half-domes themselves pushed outwards, so they placed more half-domes and arches to counterbalance them, and so on until the weight of Hagia Sophia's great dome was safely carried to the ground.

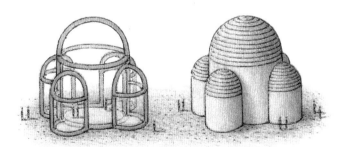

Domes and half-domes

Even so, the first dome collapsed because it was too flat. If you try to carry a heavy weight at arm's length your arm soon tires. Raise it above your head and you'll find it much easier. In the same way, a steep arch carries weight easily, while a flat one is more likely to cave in. After the collapse, the dome of Hagia Sophia was rebuilt with a deeper curve and from that day to this it has stood safe.

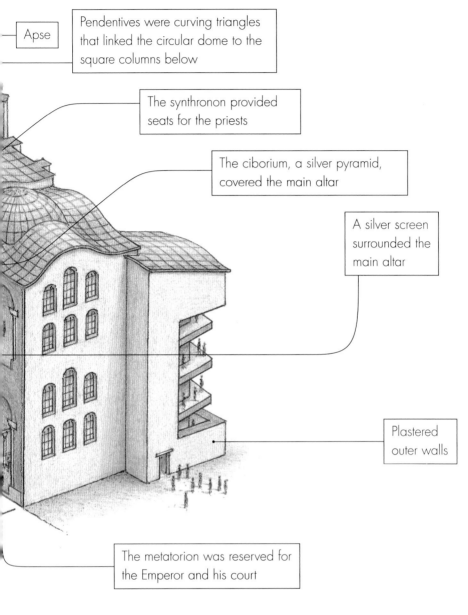

Apse

Pendentives were curving triangles that linked the circular dome to the square columns below

The synthronon provided seats for the priests

The ciborium, a silver pyramid, covered the main altar

A silver screen surrounded the main altar

Plastered outer walls

The metatorion was reserved for the Emperor and his court

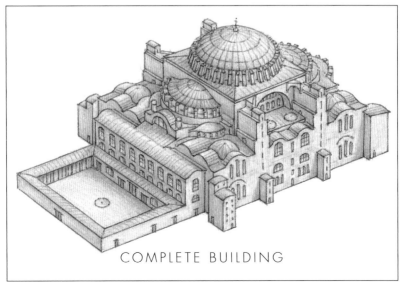

COMPLETE BUILDING

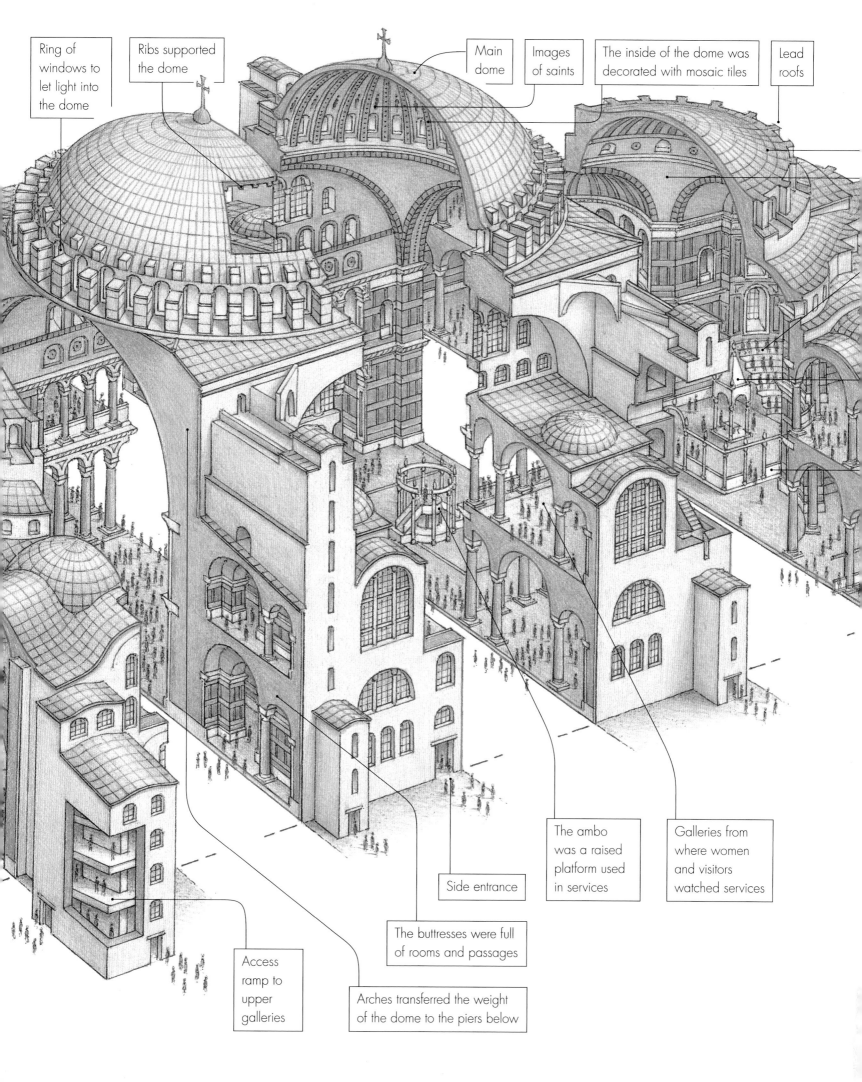

Ring of windows to let light into the dome

Ribs supported the dome

Main dome

Images of saints

The inside of the dome was decorated with mosaic tiles

Lead roofs

The ambo was a raised platform used in services

Galleries from where women and visitors watched services

Side entrance

The buttresses were full of rooms and passages

Access ramp to upper galleries

Arches transferred the weight of the dome to the piers below

A WHITE ROBE OF CHURCHES

From Hagia Sophia to Notre-Dame

The eastern part of the Roman Empire lasted for centuries before the Ottomans brought it to an end, but even as it flourished, the western part of the empire fell into decline. While Hagia Sophia was being built, ruthless fighters invaded western Europe from the forests of Germany, burning temples and sacking towns. They even destroyed Rome itself. Smoke rose into the sky as soldiers stripped gold from walls and pulled down the statues which had stared across Rome's markets for centuries.

Famine and disease followed the wars. All over western Europe, towns were deserted and farms stood empty. Weeds grew through the roads which had once crossed France, Spain and Britain. In Rome itself, houses collapsed and dogs nosed through the plants that grew over the rubble. Struggling to find food and stay alive, the few Romans who remained no longer had time to think about fine buildings. As time passed, they even forgot how to carve stone or raise domes of concrete.

By now most people in Rome were Christians. When they needed a church, they made it by dragging columns from ruins which seemed to them to have been left behind by a race of giants. Gradually they converted the invaders to their faith, until Christianity spread all over western Europe. So when, hundreds of years later, peace and order returned, the first buildings people planned were churches.

The great church at Cluny, France

which Jesus Christ had died. At its centre, stone arches rose in tiers to stone vaults that hovered over the arms of the cross like tunnels. Beyond these were lower aisles, each containing rows of altars where worshippers could pray to the different Christian saints. Inside, incense coiled up from candles on the altar, filling the church with the scent of heaven, while the monks' chanting echoed off the stone arches. The new church at Cluny was vast – most visitors had never seen a building even half so big. And as they wandered round it, everything reminded them of the Christian story. Three arches together recalled the three parts of the Christian God: Father, Son and Holy Spirit. A row of six windows reminded them of the six days God had taken to make the world.

This is what heaven will be like, thought the abbot as he looked along the church. And he saw from the faces of the worshippers that they thought so too.

Others soon copied the great church at Cluny. As peace and prosperity returned to Europe after centuries of war, monastery after monastery, city after city, built churches of the same kind. "*It was as though the very world had shaken itself,*" wrote a monk at Cluny, "*and, casting off her old age, was clothing herself everywhere in a white robe of churches.*"

Cathedrals were built all over France, and when Frenchmen from Normandy conquered England they built stone cathedrals there too. Some of the carvings were copied from old Roman columns, which is why churches of this type are called Romanesque. But mostly they were left plain. Their power came from their weighty columns and solid arches, and from the dim light that fell from tiny windows in the massive stone walls.

One town was left behind, however. In Paris, the greatest city in western Europe, people still worshipped in a shabby old cathedral that had never been rebuilt. Every time he entered it, the bishop of Paris, Maurice de Sully, felt ashamed. So he decided to build a new cathedral that would be different again from Romanesque cathedrals like Cluny. His cathedral wouldn't just impress its visitors. It would make their spirits soar.

Christians hoped that when they died they would go to heaven. The world seemed to them a poor place where people laboured and fell sick, a hard place where each dawn brought another day of work, and a summons from their king meant war and death. But they knew everything would be better when they reached God's world. What was heaven like? No one could be sure, but they pictured it as far bigger and better than anything they had ever known, a place where choirs sang and the air was filled with a heavenly fragrance.

Imagine if we built a church to show everyone what heaven will be like, thought the abbot of Cluny.

Cluny was France's richest monastery, where hundreds of monks rose each day before dawn to pray, study the Bible and worship God. The abbot decided to use its wealth to build a new kind of church, a model of heaven.

He laid the church out in the shape of the cross on

THE BISHOP'S DREAM

Notre-Dame, Cathedral of Paris, France, 1163

One morning the people of Paris were woken by the sound of falling rubble. They hurried to the island in the River Seine where their cathedral stood. And there they stopped in astonishment. Workmen were demolishing it.

Bishop Maurice stood to one side. Far from trying to stop them, he was urging them on. And when the crowd of onlookers protested, he simply shook his head.

"I'm obeying God's orders," he told them. And the bishop described a dream in which he had seen a huge new cathedral rising above Paris. He even took a stick and drew a plan on the ground to show them. When they pointed out it was too big to fit between the surrounding houses, he just shrugged.

"We'll pull the houses down," he said.

Bishop Maurice, who was a rich man, paid for the best stonemasons, the most skilled carpenters and the finest painters to be summoned from all over France. As the work gathered pace, the Parisians threw themselves into it as well. Carts rumbled over the bridges of the River Seine, streets filled with the smell of freshly-cut wood, and fires crackled under cauldrons, melting lead to seal the roofs. In dingy workshops around Paris, stonemasons tapped at carvings while artists pored over the painted glass for the windows.

Bishop Maurice spent days in discussion with the masons who were planning the cathedral. And as the

from the huge windows. Saint-Denis seemed to hang in the air by a miracle.

Bishop Maurice loved Saint-Denis and wanted Notre-Dame to be in the new style Abbot Suger had invented – the style we now call Gothic. It would be the first Gothic cathedral.

But cathedrals are enormous and building them takes years. As time passed, the stonemasons of Notre-Dame grew old and handed their hammers to their sons. Bishop Maurice grew old, but he had still not celebrated mass at its altar. Only years after his death was the cathedral finished, and only then did the people of Paris share the vision Bishop Maurice had seen in his dream.

Notre-Dame rose above the city like a mountain above a plain. Long before they reached it, travellers heard its bronze bells booming across the fields. From miles away they saw its towers, and when they reached the cathedral and went in, they felt as if they had stepped into a different world.

Stone columns soared above them like the trees of a great stone forest, while vaults danced away into the shadows. Overhead, arches pointed upwards, row after row, to huge windows whose light poured down the walls like water down a cliff face. No one had ever seen a church so tall. Far, far above its floor hung a vault of stone, pointed like a Gothic arch, with ribs that leapt from side to side like branches tossing in a high wind.

Everywhere people looked were painted windows that told stories from the Bible, or carvings describing the lives of saints. Music rose unseen from the choir beyond the screen, while the columns and arches beat a rhythm that echoed around the worshippers like a great stone hymn. No one had ever seen walls so slender or windows so large. And the stained glass of the windows, red, green and blue, coloured the light that hung over the aisles as if heaven itself had caught fire.

It felt to Notre-Dame's visitors as if Bishop Maurice really must have seen heaven in the dream he had had so many years before. Notre-Dame didn't rise ponderously, like other cathedrals. It soared.

walls of Notre-Dame rose from the ground, people began to realize how special it was going to be.

Not long before, an abbot called Suger had rebuilt part of the old church of Saint-Denis, just north of Paris, in a completely new way. Rather than strengthening the columns and walls, he had made them as slender as possible, and the windows larger than ever before. Saint-Denis wasn't dark and gloomy like other churches; light swirled around it like water playing over rocks. Abbot Suger had made another change as well. The arches of Saint-Denis were pointed, not round. Pointed arches were stronger because they didn't sag, but what Abbot Suger loved was how they pointed upwards towards heaven. The roof they supported was different as well. Instead of being round, like a tunnel, it was ribbed with lines of stone that danced in the light

NOTRE-DAME OF PARIS

Notre-Dame was the same shape as the older Romanesque cathedrals, but was far taller and lighter, with pointed arches and vaults, and stained glass windows to let in plenty of light.

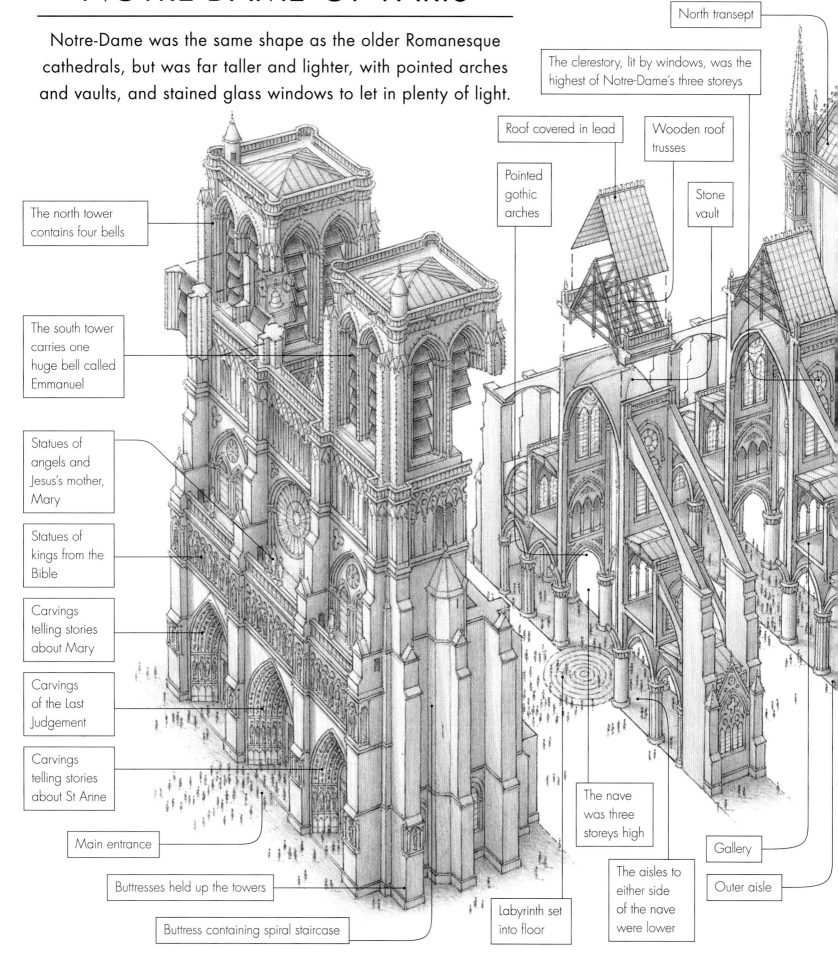

North transept

The clerestory, lit by windows, was the highest of Notre-Dame's three storeys

Roof covered in lead

Wooden roof trusses

Pointed gothic arches

Stone vault

The north tower contains four bells

The south tower carries one huge bell called Emmanuel

Statues of angels and Jesus's mother, Mary

Statues of kings from the Bible

Carvings telling stories about Mary

Carvings of the Last Judgement

Carvings telling stories about St Anne

Main entrance

Buttresses held up the towers

Buttress containing spiral staircase

Labyrinth set into floor

The nave was three storeys high

The aisles to either side of the nave were lower

Gallery

Outer aisle

THE MIDDLE AGES

Cathedrals weren't the only great buildings of the Middle Ages. Town councils built marketplaces and meeting halls to show off their wealth. Groups of merchants in the same business got together to build guildhalls, each one larger and grander than the last.

Guildhalls in Ghent, Belgium

Most of all, the Middle Ages were a time of fighting, so kings and noblemen built great castles to defend themselves and overwhelm their enemies. Castles began as simple towers, but engineers soon surrounded them with moats and outer walls, and became more and more skilful at designing bastions, barbicans, towers and drawbridges to defeat attackers. Secure in his stone castle, a nobleman could defy anybody.

A castle in the Middle Ages

GOTHIC STYLES

Notre-Dame was the first great Gothic cathedral, but in the next three hundred years, Gothic churches were built all over northern Europe and as far south as Spain. The way they changed over time can be seen from their windows.

Early Gothic lancet window

The first Gothic windows were simple pointed openings that masons built as tall as they could. Next they learnt to link windows together, sometimes twisting the tracery that supported the glass into fantastic patterns. By the end of the Middle Ages, windows spread across whole walls, clinging to networks of stone that seemed as fine as spiders' webs. The sun streamed through the stained glass windows, making the whole church glow as if it was on fire.

No one would use glass in buildings so skilfully for another four hundred years.

Window with tracery

Late Gothic windows filling a whole wall

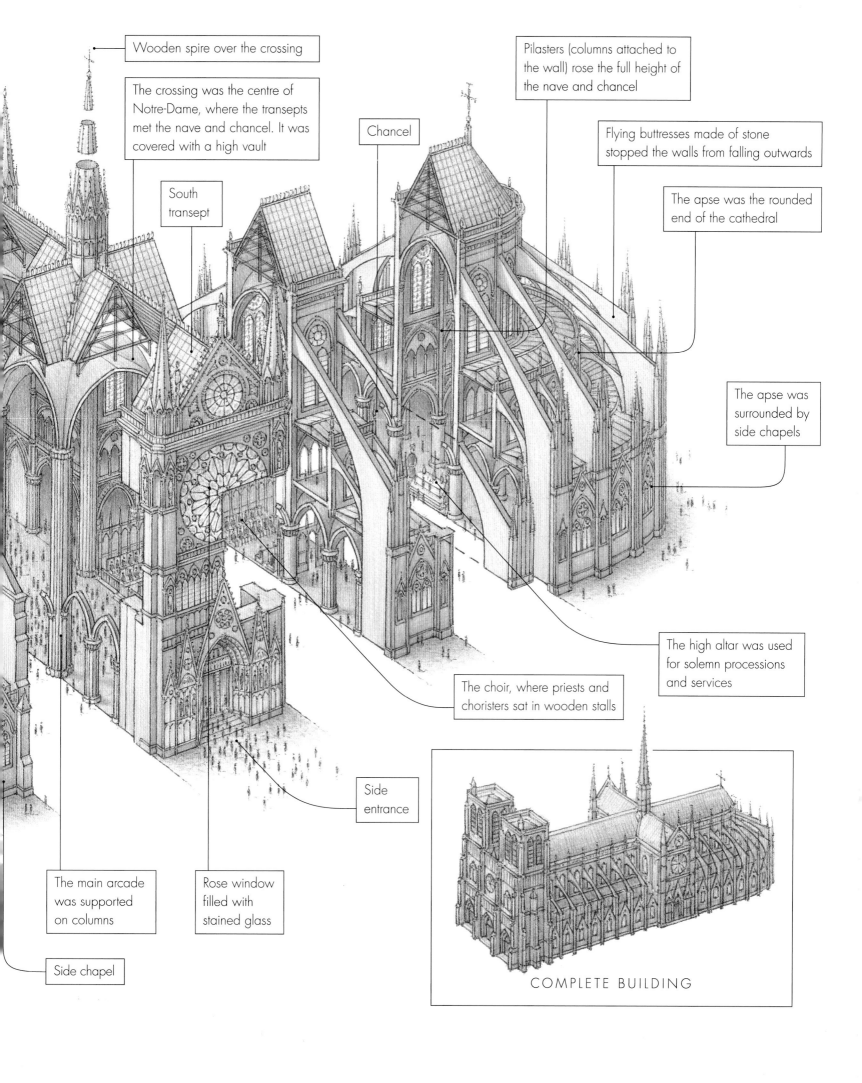

Wooden spire over the crossing

The crossing was the centre of Notre-Dame, where the transepts met the nave and chancel. It was covered with a high vault

South transept

Pilasters (columns attached to the wall) rose the full height of the nave and chancel

Chancel

Flying buttresses made of stone stopped the walls from falling outwards

The apse was the rounded end of the cathedral

The apse was surrounded by side chapels

The high altar was used for solemn processions and services

The choir, where priests and choristers sat in wooden stalls

Side entrance

The main arcade was supported on columns

Rose window filled with stained glass

Side chapel

COMPLETE BUILDING

Hindu temple at Angkor Wat, Cambodia

BUILDINGS ACROSS THE WORLD

From Notre-Dame to the Forbidden City

The Egyptians and their neighbours had been the first to build marvellous palaces, walled cities, tombs and temples. But kings all over the world wanted palaces to prove their power, while priests everywhere wanted temples to show how they respected their gods. On every continent trees were felled, stone hacked from mountains, and massive buildings rose into the air.

The first Americans built the great city of Teotihuacán, raising pyramids that could be seen from miles around. The Maya built the city of Palenque, with pyramids topped by temples and a palace for their ruler, Pacal. At Uxmal they laid out a governor's palace whose stone walls stretched as far as the eye could see, while at Cusco the Incas decorated their buildings with gold.

In India stonemasons hewed temples out of solid rock and carved fantastic shrines to Hindu gods like Vishnu and Shiva. The Indian way of building shrines spread all over the east, even as far as Angkor Wat in Cambodia, where a vast temple to the Hindu god Vishnu was crowned by spires that looked like towering clouds of stone. When European travellers visited Angkor Wat, they gazed at it in astonishment. "*It is grander than anything left to us by Greece or Rome*," one of them said.

The Arabs filled North Africa and Spain with mosques whose minarets soared up into the sky, and whose courtyards, intricately carved or decorated with tiles, replaced the city's roar with the splash of water and the murmur of prayer. Still further east, the empire of China had been united at about the time the Romans started to conquer Europe, and Chinese philosophers, scientists and inventors developed ideas that would change the world for ever.

Chinese buildings were different from buildings in

Palenque, Mexico

Mosque of Ibn Tulun, Cairo, Egypt

Europe, Africa or America. Even the grandest were made of wood. Most Chinese buildings were low, with long colonnades of wooden posts to provide shelter from the wind and sun, but sometimes they perched one storey on top of another to make high towers called pagodas. Chinese carpenters invented their own ways of jointing timber to raise roofs that curved like tree branches. Outside, the roofs were covered in brilliantly glazed tiles, while their wooden beams were carved into the faces of dragons, and painted vivid red or gold.

Indoors, Chinese houses were so comfortable they made western ones seem crude. The floors were spread with soft carpets and the walls hung with silk. They were decorated with finely-made furniture, delicate bowls and vases of porcelain so thin they were almost transparent.

Kinkaku-ji, Kyoto, Japan

The Chinese way of making buildings was copied in neighbouring countries. Korean builders made elaborate wooden temples. In Japan people didn't want fixed rooms, so their carpenters made walls with joints neat enough to be taken apart and assembled elsewhere. While Chinese builders loved grandeur, the Japanese preferred their buildings plain. Wood was beautiful enough in itself, they thought; it didn't need paint or decoration. They laid plain rice mats on their floors, and fitted their walls with sliding screens that opened to reveal beautiful gardens. To the Japanese a house was somewhere to escape the troubles of the world, a place of calm and contemplation.

No one needed to escape the world's cares as much as Shogun Ashikaga Yoshimitsu, who ruled Japan on behalf of the emperor. All day long he worked, reading reports and meeting his advisers. At night he returned to his estate exhausted and sat by the side of a little lake where trees swept the water with their leaves. There he felt his strength return. It was his favourite place on earth, and every night he grew sad when it became too cold to stay out. So when he retired, Ashikaga Yoshimitsu decided to build a pavilion there. He didn't need a proper house with kitchens and bedrooms; just a room where he could watch the lake. And so the Kinkaku-ji, or Golden Pavilion, took shape. The Kinkaku-ji was as calm as the water that reflected its slender columns and delicate balconies, as elegant as the rushes that bowed to each gust of wind. As the sun dipped towards the horizon each evening, Ashikaga Yoshimitsu sat on its balconies and felt all his cares fall away.

At much the same time, the ruler of China decided he wanted a very different building – one that would show the world how powerful he was. China was the largest country on earth, so when Zhu Di, the Yongle Emperor, third ruler of the Ming Dynasty, planned a new palace in Beijing, he didn't build a delicate pavilion.

He built a whole city.

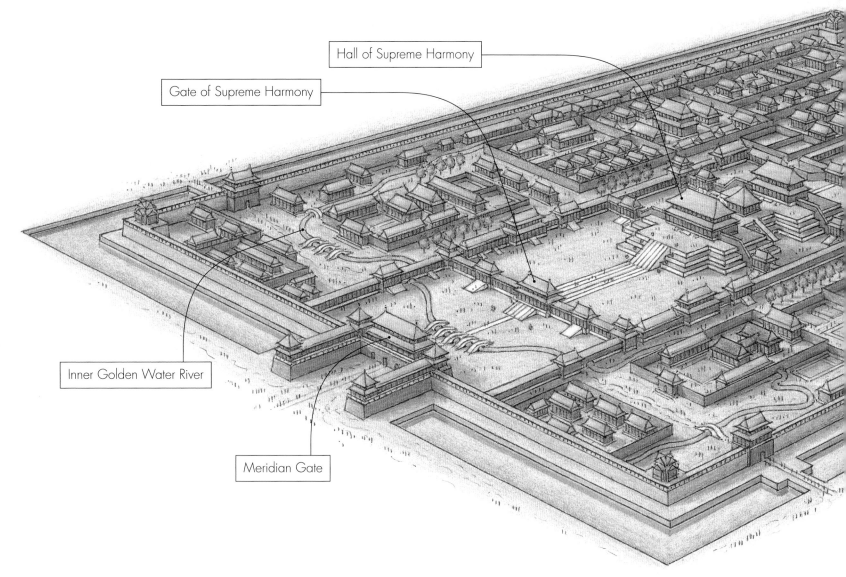

Hall of Supreme Harmony
Gate of Supreme Harmony
Inner Golden Water River
Meridian Gate

THE FORBIDDEN CITY

Zijin Cheng, Beijing, China, 1406

The emperor Zhu Di called his palace Zijin Cheng: the Forbidden City. No one could enter it unless invited. Nothing happened there except by his command.

A moat fifty metres wide surrounded the Forbidden City, its walls were as tall as a house, and each corner was crowned with a tower. The walls were painted red, the colour of good fortune. In each was a gate from where a road, long and straight, set out through the Imperial City, through the city of Beijing, and out to the furthest corners of China.

In every town, every village, every field in China, Zhu Di's word was law. Enthroned in the Forbidden City he would snap out an order, horsemen would set off,

and thousands of miles away a man would be arrested, a minister sacked or a family covered in wealth. To the Chinese the Forbidden City was the centre of the universe, and when visitors arrived there, dusty from their long journeys, Zhu Di wanted them to find a perfect world, a miniature China, a place whose order and harmony explained why he had taken the title of Yongle, the Emperor of Perpetual Happiness.

Entering through the Meridian Gate, visitors found themselves in a vast courtyard. Across it ran a waterway, the Inner Golden Water River, which meandered right through the Forbidden City. Five bridges faced them. They had to cross one to reach the Taihemen, the Gate

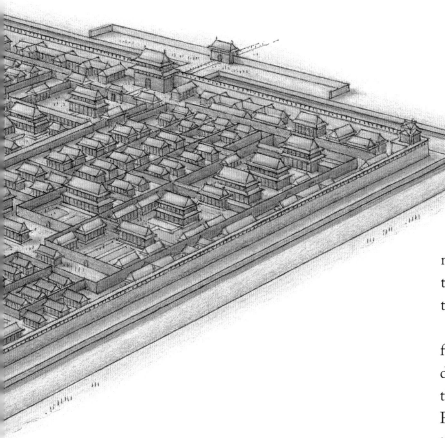

of Supreme Harmony, which led to the emperor's inner courtyard. By the time they reached the Taihemen, most were already trembling with fear. When they passed through it, they fell to their knees in awe. For beyond the Taihemen, on a high terrace of marble, stood the Taihedian, or Hall of Supreme Harmony, where the emperor's throne stood under a ceiling decorated with a coiled dragon.

Past the Taihedian were more great halls, while all around it lay more courtyards, more colonnades and more palaces. Each had its purpose; each had a name. One was the Hall of Military Eminence, another, the Hall of Literary Glory, for everything in China had its reflection in the Forbidden City of the Yongle Emperor. Unseen to most visitors, there were still more courtyards beyond, where the emperor himself lived in the Palace of Heavenly Purity, and his empress in the Palace of Earthly Tranquillity.

For generations, emperors ruled China from behind the walls of the Forbidden City. They never saw the people they governed. Courtiers arrived at the gates; armies set off for wars far away. But inside the city nothing changed. Fabulous banquets were served from the kitchens. Servants prostrated themselves before the throne. It was as if time stood still.

Yet no power lasts for ever, even though rulers try to fix it in stone. Armies are defeated; emperors fall. The descendants of the Emperor of Perpetual Happiness lost their throne, and another dynasty took their place in the Forbidden City. Still the Golden Water River flowed through the courtyards; still the trees blossomed in the imperial gardens; but China itself grew less powerful. The world changed; foreign soldiers arrived; generals began to squabble and fight. Emperors sent instructions from the Forbidden City but no one obeyed them any more. They ordered armies into battle – but no longer had armies to command. Other people ruled China and, entombed within the Forbidden City, the Chinese emperors never realized that their power was gone.

The last emperor of all was just a boy. His servants told him he ruled the whole of China, but he didn't know what China looked like – he had never been outside the walls of his palace. One day the servants left. He stood beyond the Hall of Supreme Harmony and watched them go, filing out through the Taihemen. Afterwards he ran round the palace alone. He stood on the marble bridges of the waterway. He sat on his throne under the coiled dragon. Like a pea rattling inside a drum he wandered through empty halls and abandoned corridors.

Zhu Di had dreamt of a palace that would dominate the whole world. The palace remained, but the dream had come to an end.

The roofs were decorated with fish and other water creatures. They were supposed to protect the palace from fire

A coiled dragon was carved above the Emperor's throne

Imperial throne

The Hall of Supreme Harmony was the heart of the Forbidden City

Everything around the Emperor's throne was decorated gold

The Hall of Central Harmony was used for resting between ceremonies

Imperial throne

Massive wooden columns held up the roofs

Bronze cauldrons held water to put out fires

Soldiers and servants always surrounded the Emperor

The central ramp was only used by the Emperor

CANTILEVERS

Instead of using trusses, Chinese carpenters invented their own way of building roofs to cover great halls, courts and meeting rooms. Fitting each piece of wood together with an intricate joint, they balanced beam on beam to make cantilevers, which jutted out from the posts that supported them, and rose higher and higher until they met in the middle.

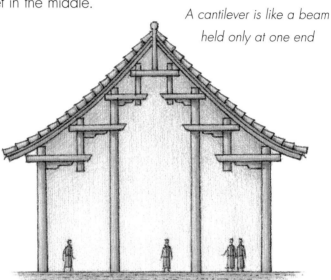

A cantilever is like a beam held only at one end

Chinese hall using cantilevers to support the roof

Much later, people all over the world would realize how strong cantilevers were and use the same principle to construct vast structures like the Forth Bridge in Scotland and the Quebec Bridge in Canada.

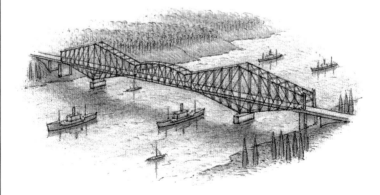

Quebec Bridge, Canada

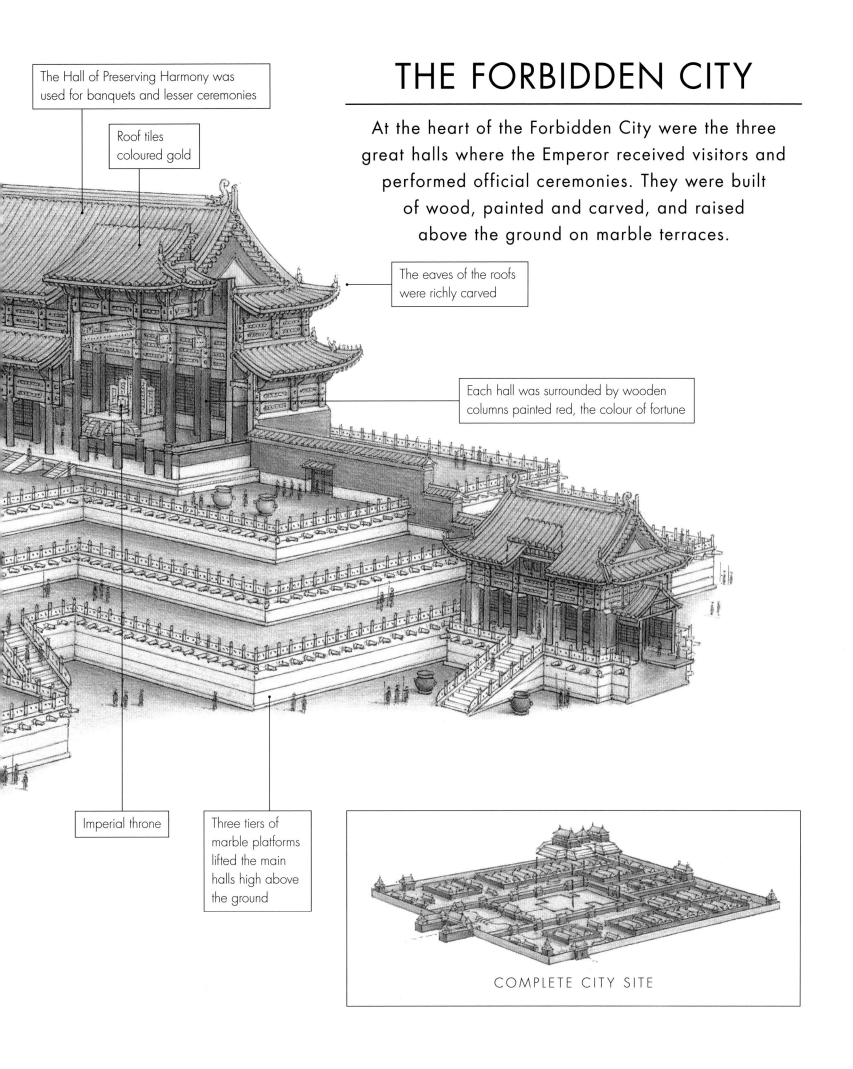

THE FORBIDDEN CITY

At the heart of the Forbidden City were the three great halls where the Emperor received visitors and performed official ceremonies. They were built of wood, painted and carved, and raised above the ground on marble terraces.

The Hall of Preserving Harmony was used for banquets and lesser ceremonies

Roof tiles coloured gold

The eaves of the roofs were richly carved

Each hall was surrounded by wooden columns painted red, the colour of fortune

Imperial throne

Three tiers of marble platforms lifted the main halls high above the ground

COMPLETE CITY SITE

THE RENAISSANCE IN EUROPE

From the Forbidden City to Villa Rotonda

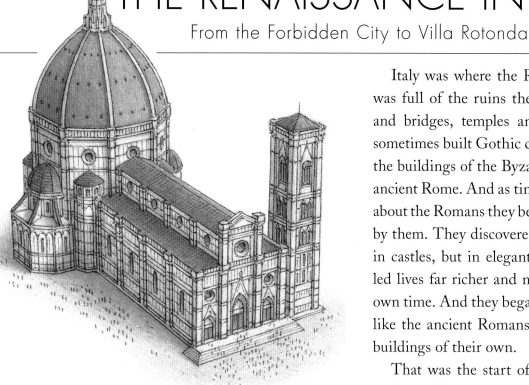

Brunelleschi's dome, Florence

In western Europe people built Gothic churches, castles and cathedrals for hundreds of years. Every town competed to come up with the most magnificent building. In France the cathedrals of Chartres, Rheims and Amiens soared into the sky, and in each the vaults were higher, and windows bigger. The people of Chartres were so eager to build their cathedral that when they had no horses to pull their carts, they grabbed the harnesses and dragged stone to the building site with their bare hands.

Sometimes, as ideas changed, parts of churches would be pulled down and rebuilt in a new way. Sometimes things went wrong and the walls crashed to the ground in clouds of dust. In those days, engineers didn't know how to calculate the weights and forces in a building, so they had to work by experiment. Gradually, though, they learnt to make walls thinner, to balance the weight of vaults with flying buttresses, and to raise stone spires so slender they pierced the clouds like arrows. But at about the time the Forbidden City was being built in faraway China, there was a change in the way Europeans built. And it began in Italy.

Italy was where the Romans had come from, and it was full of the ruins they had left behind – aqueducts and bridges, temples and theatres. Although Italians sometimes built Gothic churches, and sometimes copied the buildings of the Byzantines, they never forgot about ancient Rome. And as time went by and they learnt more about the Romans they became more and more fascinated by them. They discovered that the Romans hadn't lived in castles, but in elegant palaces and villas where they led lives far richer and more stylish than those of their own time. And they began to dream that they might live like the ancient Romans themselves, and build Roman buildings of their own.

That was the start of what we call the Renaissance or "rebirth" of classical (meaning Greek and Roman) ideas. But when the architects of the Renaissance tried to copy Roman buildings they found they didn't have much to go on. They knew the Romans used round, not

Alberti's church of Sant' Andrea, Mantua

Bramante's Tempietto San Pietro, Rome

pointed, arches; and they knew about the orders of classical architecture: Doric, Ionic and Corinthian. They had a book about buildings by a Roman architect called Vitruvius (although a lot of it was about bridges and military camps). They visited Rome to see temples like the Pantheon. But most of the buildings the Romans had left were in ruins. Renaissance architects were a bit like cooks with all the right ingredients but no recipe.

So they set about inventing classical buildings all over again. In Florence an architect called Filippo Brunelleschi put a Roman-style dome on the new cathedral, and designed simple churches with classical arches. Another architect, Leon Battista Alberti, wrote a book about classical architecture and designed a church in Mantua with a front that looked like a Roman arch. A third, Donato Bramante, went to Rome and built classical palaces and a little round temple in the Roman style. And the pope decided to rebuild the great cathedral of St Peter's in Rome in the classical style too.

One day classical architecture would take over from Gothic and spread all over the world. But before that could happen, someone had to work out how to use it not only for palaces and churches but for all kinds of buildings. The person who did that was a stonemason called Andrea Palladio from a little town in Italy called Vicenza.

And he did it not by making classical buildings richer or more ornate, but by making them as simple as possible.

THE PERFECT HOUSE
Villa Rotonda, Vicenza, Italy, 1567

Vicenza was near the great trading city of Venice, and its leading citizens grew wealthy selling the Venetians food from their farms. But unlike Venice, which was full of beautiful buildings, Vicenza was small and ugly.

"Full of farmers," most people sneered when anyone mentioned it.

That made the noblemen of Vicenza furious. They may have owned farms, but they also tried hard to stay in touch with the latest ideas. They studied ancient Greek and Roman books; and as they sat together under the stars, drinking their wine, they discussed the very things that had fascinated Greeks and Romans so many centuries before. How do you make things beautiful? Can something perfect be made on earth, or is perfection only an idea? Can you make a perfect statue? Can you make a perfect house?

One of the noblemen, Gian Giorgio Trissino, was rebuilding his own house and noticed that his best stonemason, Andrea della Gondola, often joined them to listen to their discussions. Andrea had read all the books on classical buildings and learnt how to copy classical carvings. Trissino decided to send him to Rome to study the ruins for himself. But before he left, Trissino gave him a new name. He called him Andrea Palladio after the Greek goddess of wisdom, Pallas Athena.

In Rome Palladio spent his days drawing and studying. By measuring old columns he rediscovered the subtle calculations that made them look just right. He found that even the simple carvings around doors or windows had carefully worked-out measurements that obeyed mathematical rules. Classical architecture wasn't only about the different orders, he realized; it was about maths. He drew the plans of ancient houses and temples and learnt that classical buildings were symmetrical, which meant one side was a perfect mirror image of the other. The best rooms were perfect squares and circles. If they were rectangular, the proportion of width to length was carefully worked out. And as he worked at his sketchbook day after day, Palladio came to a conclusion. Buildings didn't have to be decorated with elaborate columns, arches or statues to be beautiful. What really mattered was the relation of each part to the others. If you made them symmetrical and used maths to balance each part with the whole, you could make them as simple as you liked.

Back home in Vicenza, Palladio started designing country houses for the noblemen. They couldn't all afford elaborate carvings, but he made their villas simple, symmetrical and perfectly proportioned. Soon Palladio was asked to improve the city of Vicenza as well, so he filled the streets with palaces, and covered the shabby old government building with tiers of classical arches. Instead of being a poor market town, Vicenza became one of the most beautiful cities in the world.

One day, Palladio had a visitor from Rome: a priest, Paolo Almerico, who told him that he had decided to move to Vicenza. He had bought a hill outside the city and on it he wanted Palladio to build him the perfect house.

How often had Palladio and the others argued about the idea of a perfect house? Most people said it wasn't possible to make something perfect out of rough bricks and wood. Only ideas could be perfect, not things. Could you make a building out of an idea?

Palladio took a piece of paper and drew a square on it. Wasn't the circle, the simplest shape of all, also the most perfect? He drew a circle within the square. Paolo Almerico's house would be perfect in shape – a circle within a square. The centre would be a circular hall; each side would have a porch looking out over the beautiful landscape of Vicenza. The outside walls wouldn't need elaborate decoration; they were better without it. By keeping Paolo Almerico's house pure and simple, Palladio had made his most beautiful villa of all.

One thing troubled him, though. How many people would ever travel to Vicenza to see his perfect villa? How many people would go to Rome and study for themselves until they learnt the secrets of proportion and symmetry? So Palladio decided to put his work into a book. He and his assistants drew Paolo Almerico's villa – the plan that showed its layout, the elevations that described each side, and a section that cut it open like a doll's house. They drew every building he had ever designed. Painstakingly they drew the monuments he had visited in Rome, the best carvings for windows, the strongest ways to build a wall. By the time they had finished, their drawings filled four volumes.

Palladio's *Four Books of Architecture* were published all over Europe. In France and Germany, Spain and Britain, people pored over the drawings and copied them. Palladio's designs were so simple that anyone could use them. By following his rules, they could make beautiful buildings from materials as cheap as brick and plaster. And as they studied the designs of Paolo Almerico's house, they understood for themselves what Palladio had discovered as he sat among the ruins of Rome.

Beauty doesn't depend on rich decoration. The simplest things can be the most perfect.

SYMMETRY

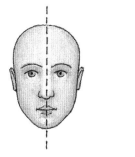 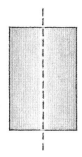

Lines of symmetry

Your face is symmetrical. If you look at the two sides of your face, you'll see that one is a mirror image of the other. Mark a rectangle on a piece of paper and you can draw a line of symmetry that divides it into two exactly equal halves. Classical architects always tried to make their buildings symmetrical, as Palladio did.

You can add a second line of symmetry to a square or rectangle, cutting it not just into equal halves but equal quarters. Circles are completely symmetrical. By designing his villa around a circle inside a square, with a porch on each side, Palladio made a building that was perfectly balanced.

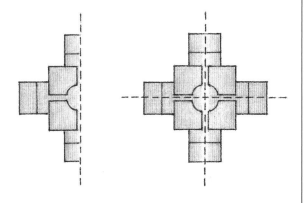

Villa Rotonda's lines of symmetry

VILLA ROTONDA

The Villa Rotonda wasn't meant to be lived in all the time. It was designed for visits, festivals and parties.

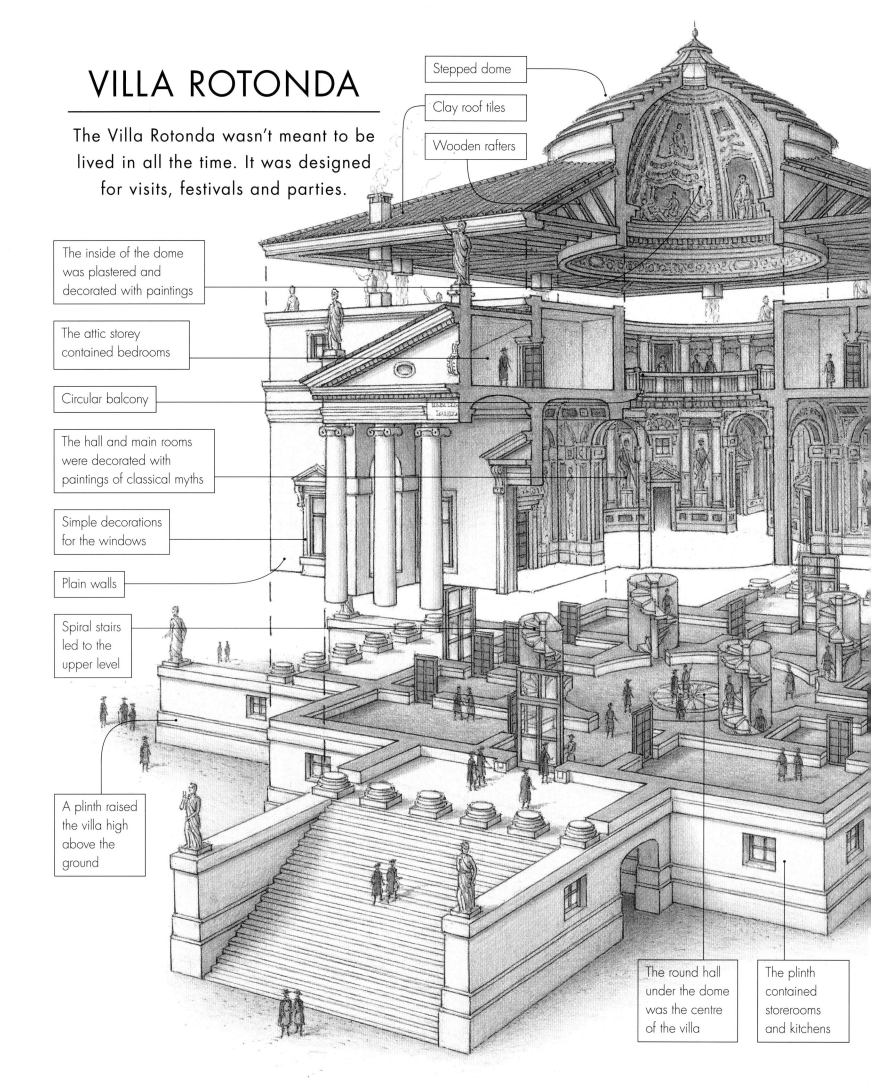

Stepped dome

Clay roof tiles

Wooden rafters

The inside of the dome was plastered and decorated with paintings

The attic storey contained bedrooms

Circular balcony

The hall and main rooms were decorated with paintings of classical myths

Simple decorations for the windows

Plain walls

Spiral stairs led to the upper level

A plinth raised the villa high above the ground

The round hall under the dome was the centre of the villa

The plinth contained storerooms and kitchens

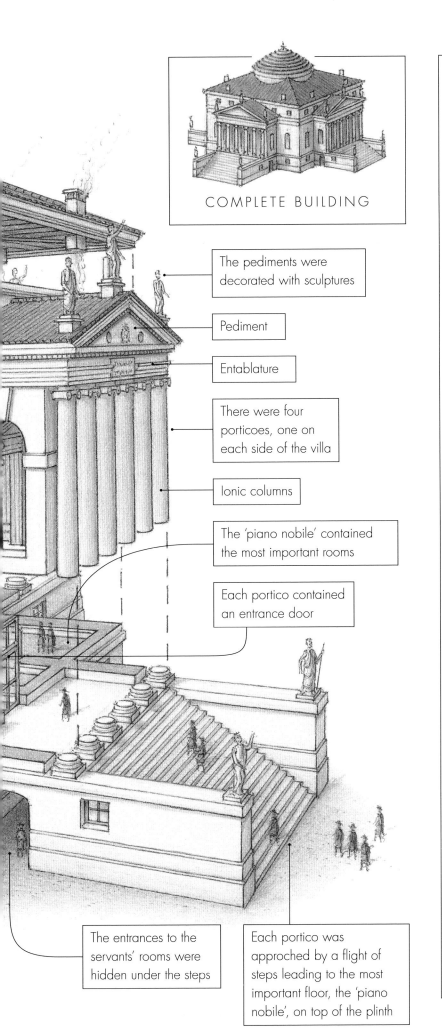

COMPLETE BUILDING

The pediments were decorated with sculptures

Pediment

Entablature

There were four porticoes, one on each side of the villa

Ionic columns

The 'piano nobile' contained the most important rooms

Each portico contained an entrance door

The entrances to the servants' rooms were hidden under the steps

Each portico was approched by a flight of steps leading to the most important floor, the 'piano nobile', on top of the plinth

GEOMETRY

Renaissance architects used geometry and mathematics to plan their buildings. Each part of the building was a mathematical shape like a square or rectangle, and the whole building needed to be a geometric shape as well.

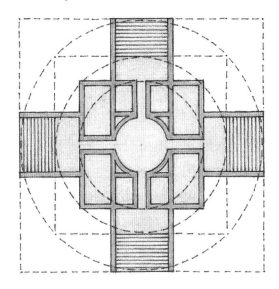

The plan of Villa Rotonda

People during the Renaissance believed that mathematics contained the secret of pure beauty, and things only looked right when they reflected mathematical proportions. Mathematics linked everything together; ideas, buildings – and people.

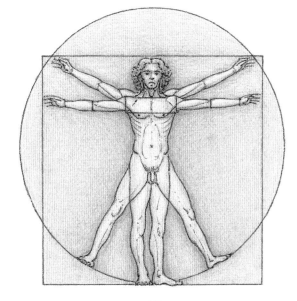

THE EMPEROR'S GRIEF

The Taj Mahal, Agra, India, 1632

Western Europeans weren't the only ones to seek perfection in their buildings. They weren't the only ones to use symmetry and geometry. The temples built by the Maya and Incas in South America were symmetrical. So were Hindu buildings like the temple at Angkor Wat. Muslim mathematicians were famous for their skill, and Muslim architects devised systems of proportion that made each part of their buildings seem perfectly balanced against the others.

After the Ottomans conquered Byzantium, their great architect Mimar Sinan, who lived about the same time as Andrea Palladio, designed mosques that were exactly symmetrical, with a dome at the centre and a minaret – a tower for calling people to prayer – at each corner. After Hagia Sophia was turned into a mosque, Ottoman engineers became expert at building domes for themselves, and spread their knowledge across the Muslim world. At Isfahan, in Iran, the domes of the mosques towered above the desert and could be seen from miles away by travellers making the long journey from China to Europe. The dome of the largest mosque, the Masjid-i-Shah, rose 53 metres into the air and was covered with gleaming blue and green tiles.

Northern India was conquered by Muslim rulers known as the Mughals. The Mughals admired the skill at stone-carving that Indians used to decorate Hindu temples. But they also brought with them the Muslim love of mathematics and geometry, and just outside Delhi, their capital, they used them to make a building still more perfectly balanced than the villa Andrea Palladio had built for Paolo Almerico. Like the Villa Rotonda it was designed around a dome above a square, and was symmetrical in every way. Like the Rotonda it seemed to hover above the ground as if it came from another world. But it wasn't a pleasure-house. It was a tomb.

The Emperor Shah Jahan was the fiercest and most powerful of all the Mughal rulers. Every year his soldiers conquered more territory and the poets at his court sang of more battles and more victories. The treasure in Shah Jahan's cellars was piled so high no one could count it. But although kings envied Shah Jahan and armies trembled at his name, Shah Jahan cared for only one thing: the love of his wife, who was so beautiful that he called her Mumtaz Mahal, the Jewel of the Palace.

When Mumtaz Mahal fell ill and died, Shah Jahan was heartbroken. And he ordered his architects to build a tomb worthy of the love he felt for her.

Sculptors were summoned from all over India. Elephants dragged blocks of marble across the plains. Above the River Yamuna, workmen dug canals and raised a huge platform of white marble for the tomb.

At each corner of the platform stood a slender minaret. At the centre rose white marble walls pierced by arches and inlaid with precious stones. The four walls of the tomb were identical, with a giant arched doorway at the centre of each. Inside was an octagonal chamber with an entrance in each wall and an arch above each entrance. The tomb stood at the centre of the chamber. And exactly above it rose the huge dome of white marble that hovered over the body of Mumtaz Mahal like a marble moon.

Every wall was decorated with carvings, jewels or inlaid stone, with flowers, patterns or holy texts. When the rising sun touched the dome it seemed to glow with its own inner light.

The tomb was called the Taj Mahal. Around it Shah Jahan laid out gardens filled with streams and ponds so that, wherever he walked, he could see the reflection of the Taj Mahal and remember his dead wife.

"The sight of this mansion creates sorrowing sighs," he wrote. *"And the sun and the moon shed tears from their eyes."*

And he would stare at his wife's tomb and think of the day when he would die in his turn and finally be laid alongside Mumtaz Mahal, the Jewel of the Palace.

PATTERN

Muslims were forbidden by their religion from making pictures of people so Muslim designers became experts at patterns instead. Sometimes the patterns were intricate geometric shapes; sometimes they followed the swirling forms of plants and leaves. The Ottomans painted patterns onto ceramic tiles which they baked in kilns until their colours shone like precious jewels. When the sun was at its hottest, people could go into courtyards filled with cool blue and green tiles as if they were entering a garden.

Iznik tile

At the Taj Mahal, Indian stonemasons, who were famous for their craftsmanship, used different techniques to decorate Mumtaz Mahal's tomb. In some places they carved designs into the stone. In others they scratched lines and rubbed paint into them. In others again, they cut out grooves in the white marble and fitted tiny slivers of coloured stone into them to make a pattern. They used the same technique to write the lines from the Quran, the Muslim holy book, which covered the walls of the tomb.

Frieze from the Taj Mahal

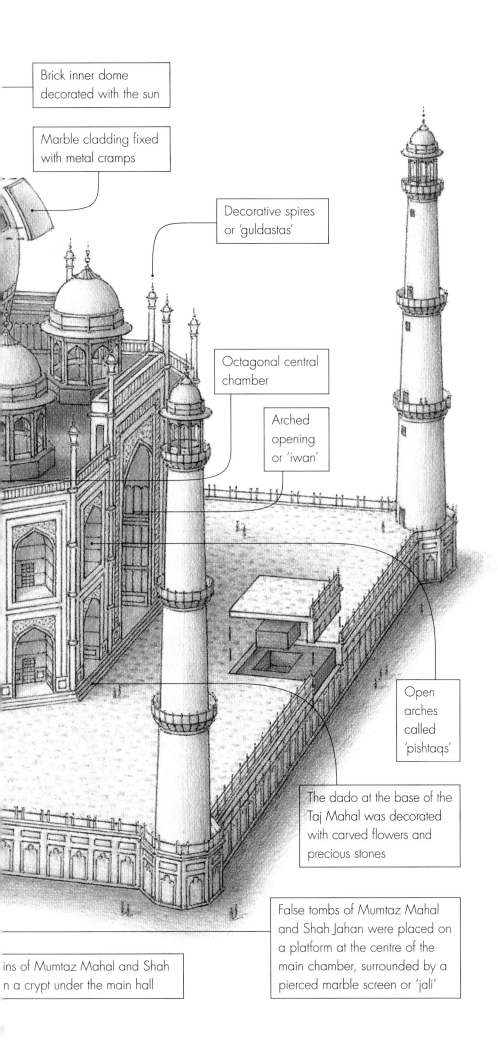

Brick inner dome decorated with the sun

Marble cladding fixed with metal cramps

Decorative spires or 'guldastas'

Octagonal central chamber

Arched opening or 'iwan'

Open arches called 'pishtaqs'

The dado at the base of the Taj Mahal was decorated with carved flowers and precious stones

False tombs of Mumtaz Mahal and Shah Jahan were placed on a platform at the centre of the main chamber, surrounded by a pierced marble screen or 'jali'

ins of Mumtaz Mahal and Shah n a crypt under the main hall

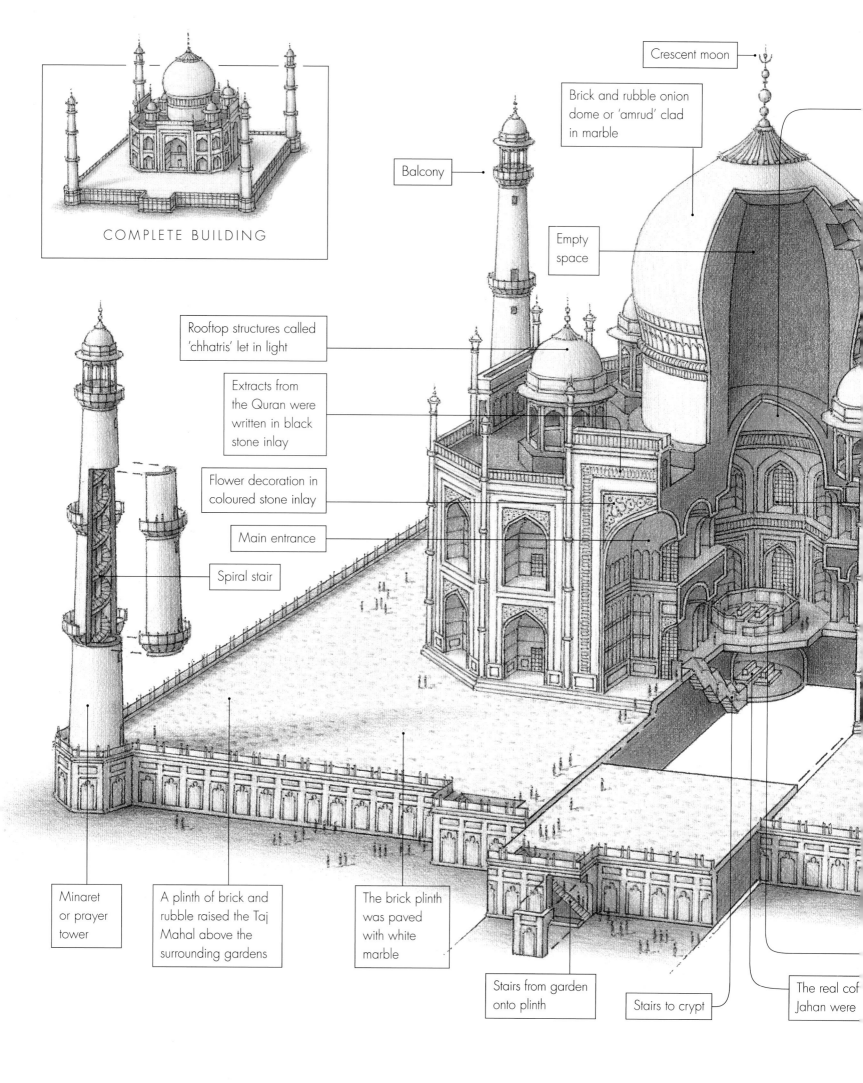

COMPLETE BUILDING

Crescent moon

Brick and rubble onion dome or 'amrud' clad in marble

Balcony

Empty space

Rooftop structures called 'chhatris' let in light

Extracts from the Quran were written in black stone inlay

Flower decoration in coloured stone inlay

Main entrance

Spiral stair

Minaret or prayer tower

A plinth of brick and rubble raised the Taj Mahal above the surrounding gardens

The brick plinth was paved with white marble

Stairs from garden onto plinth

Stairs to crypt

The real cof Jahan were

THE BAROQUE IN EUROPE
From the Taj Mahal to Vaux-le-Vicomte

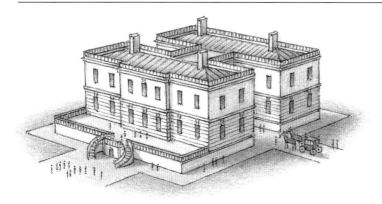

The Queen's House, London

With the help of Andrea Palladio's *Four Books of Architecture*, classical buildings spread all over Europe. No one wanted Gothic arches any more; they wanted their houses and churches to look classical. So stonemasons learned how to carve the rams' horns of Ionic columns and the acanthus leaves of Corinthian columns, and buildings became square and symmetrical in the classical way.

But whereas Andrea Palladio had loved simplicity, it wasn't long before designers started using classical columns, arches and domes to make buildings wilder and more dramatic than any seen since the days of the Gothic cathedrals. At that time the great kings of Europe were

becoming richer and more powerful. They weren't interested in simplicity. They wanted palaces that would fill their subjects with awe. The Christian church had been divided by a great argument called the Reformation, and the Pope, leader of the Catholics, wanted churches so breathtaking that worshippers would fall to their knees in wonder. And it was in Rome, where the Pope lived, that the change began.

The architects of Rome outdid each other in inventing fantastic shapes. Instead of circles and squares, they designed their buildings as ovals, triangles and spirals. They made carvings as complicated as possible, covered walls with multicoloured marbles and doorways with figures, filled their churches with candles and built domes that soared into the sky above Rome. Classical columns were supposed to be evenly spaced. Roman designers grouped them in pairs, or placed one on top of another as if hundreds of columns were bursting from a single block of stone. Classical columns rose straight and tall from base to capital; Roman columns spiralled upwards like stone corkscrews.

The two most famous architects in Rome were called

Gian Lorenzo Bernini and Francesco Borromini, and they were deadly rivals. Bernini was rich and Borromini poor. Bernini was charming; Borromini surly and ill-tempered. Bernini had friends among all the lords of Rome while Borromini lived alone, working obsessively into the night. The two men hated each other.

Bernini surrounded the great church of St Peter's with a huge square bounded by curving rows of columns. Borromini built small, dark churches whose strange shapes and obsessive patterns made people whisper that he was going mad. A story is often told of how the rivalry between the two architects came to a head. In Rome's grandest piazza Borromini built a church with a curving front and a dome that hung over it like the face of a cliff. Bernini was asked to design a fountain in the middle of the piazza. On it he carved a stone figure recoiling from Borromini's church in horror.

The new buildings weren't simple, like Renaissance ones, so people called them baroque after the Portuguese word for a pearl that isn't quite perfect, but is all the more beautiful for its flaws. They were the most fanciful anyone could remember. And it wasn't only the Romans who loved them. When London burned down in a great fire, Christopher Wren rebuilt the cathedral, St Paul's, in the baroque way and filled the skyline with baroque spires.

Piazza Navona, Rome

The Spanish had conquered South America and built baroque cathedrals to awe their new subjects with the power of the Christian God. And kings in Europe started to dream of baroque palaces that would awe their subjects too. The most powerful king of all was Louis XIV of France. But the first baroque palace in France was not built by him. To his fury, it was built by one of his subjects.

St Peter's square, Rome

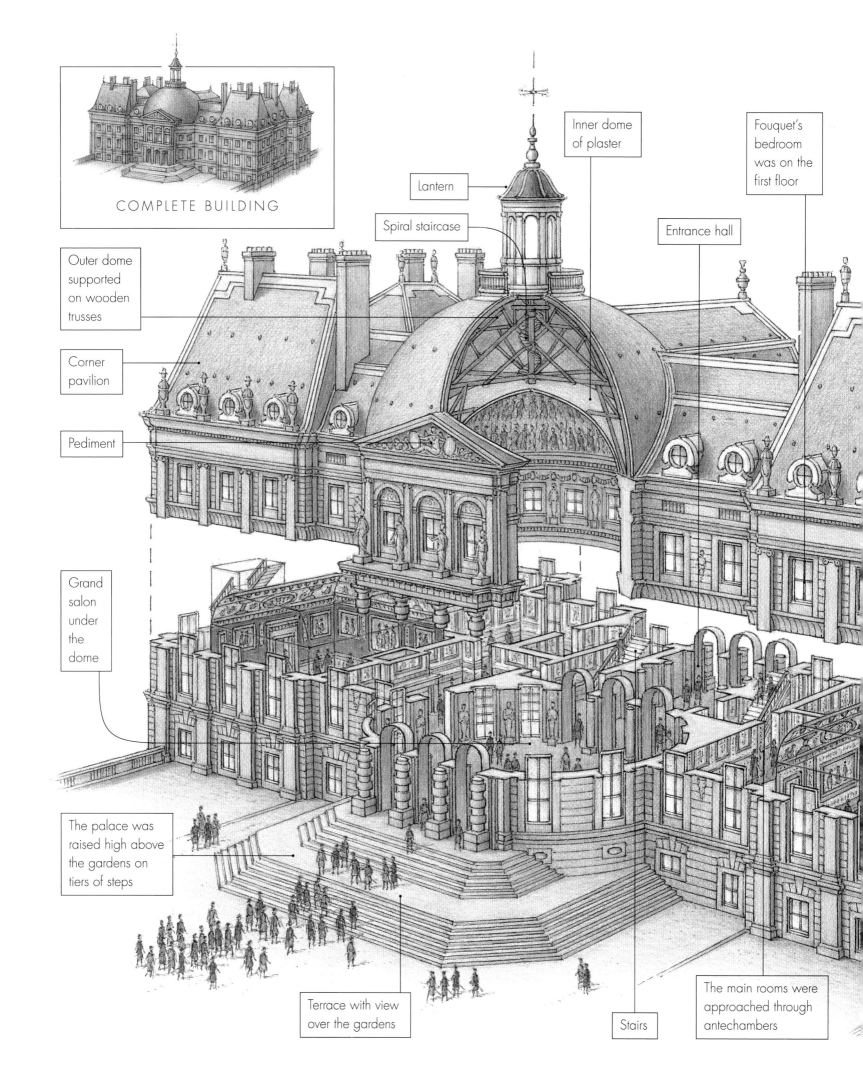

COMPLETE BUILDING

Lantern

Inner dome of plaster

Fouquet's bedroom was on the first floor

Spiral staircase

Entrance hall

Outer dome supported on wooden trusses

Corner pavilion

Pediment

Grand salon under the dome

The palace was raised high above the gardens on tiers of steps

Terrace with view over the gardens

Stairs

The main rooms were approached through antechambers

THE RICHEST MAN IN FRANCE

Vaux-le-Vicomte, France, 1657

The attic contained rooms for servants and visitors

The richest man in France was the king's minister of finance, Nicolas Fouquet. Fouquet wasn't a duke or count, but he decided to build a house that would put every palace in France to shame.

He bought an estate outside Paris called Vaux-le-Vicomte and hired the best designers in the country. Louis Le Vau would design the palace, Charles Le Brun would decorate it, and André Le Nôtre would lay out the gardens. Fouquet didn't stop to think that the king, Louis XIV, might be jealous. When the palace was finished he announced the grandest opening party France had ever seen. Molière, the most famous writer in the world, was commissioned to write a special play for the occasion. The greatest chef in France was appointed to prepare the dinner for a thousand guests. The terraces of Vaux-le-Vicomte were filled with musicians, footmen handed out trays of champagne, and at midnight a fireworks display lit up the sky. Everyone wore fancy dress, but Fouquet wore the most splendid costume of all.

King Louis was one of the guests. He didn't smile as Fouquet greeted him. His own costume was nothing like as splendid as his minister's and, by comparison with Vaux-le-Vicomte, his palaces were shabby and old-fashioned. As Fouquet showed off gardens and marble-lined rooms, the king's face grew more and more grim. Too late, Fouquet realized his mistake and tried to soothe Louis, but the king stormed out in a fury. Nicolas Fouquet was ruined.

"At six in the evening Fouquet was like the King of France," the famous writer Voltaire said. *"At two in the morning he was nobody!"*

Fouquet was arrested and thrown in jail, where he died nineteen years later. But his palace of Vaux-le-Vicomte was not forgotten, for it gave King Louis an idea. He summoned the designers of Vaux-le-Vicomte and ordered them to start work on a new palace for him at Versailles, outside Paris. Versailles was even larger than Vaux-le-Vicomte. Its gardens spread even further; the feasts held in them were still more magnificent. Louis had always wanted his subjects to obey him and his rivals to fear him. His new palace displayed his power for all to see. When noblemen came to Versailles they knew there was no chance of challenging the king. When foreign ambassadors saw its pavilions they gave up opposing France. With Versailles as his home, Louis grew more and more powerful, until everyone recognized him as the greatest monarch in Europe.

Fouquet's main room: the Chamber of the Muses

The basement contained kitchens and storerooms

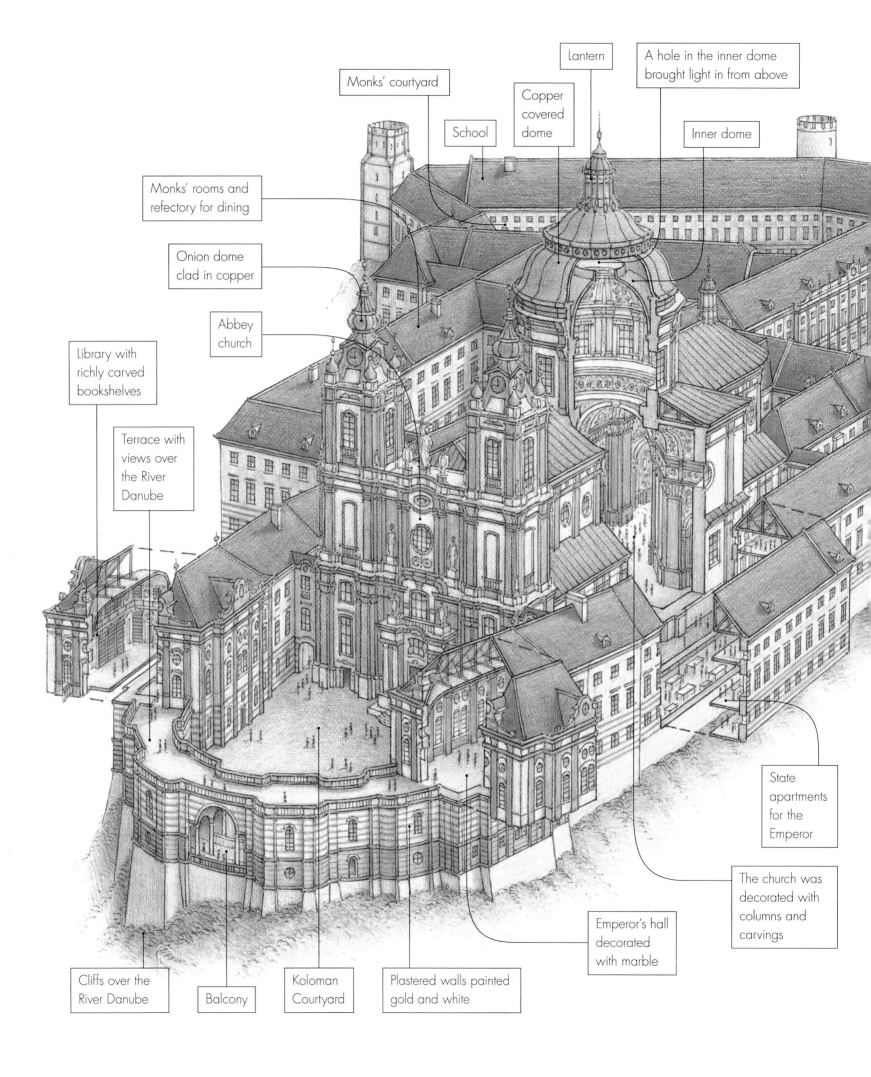

Monks' courtyard

Lantern

A hole in the inner dome brought light in from above

School

Copper covered dome

Inner dome

Monks' rooms and refectory for dining

Onion dome clad in copper

Abbey church

Library with richly carved bookshelves

Terrace with views over the River Danube

State apartments for the Emperor

The church was decorated with columns and carvings

Cliffs over the River Danube

Balcony

Koloman Courtyard

Plastered walls painted gold and white

Emperor's hall decorated with marble

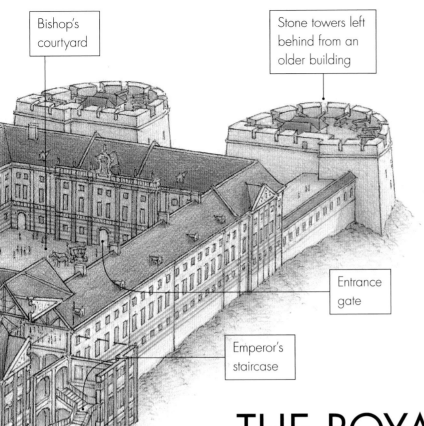

Bishop's courtyard

Stone towers left behind from an older building

Entrance gate

Emperor's staircase

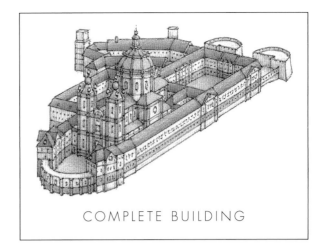

COMPLETE BUILDING

THE ROYAL ABBEY

Melk Abbey, Austria, 1702

Louis XIV of France had shown how a building could display the power of a king. Other European emperors and kings soon copied him, and baroque palaces appeared all over Europe, with twisting staircases, writhing columns, and walls that curved in and out like waves crashing on a beach. Gilded plasterwork unfurled across ceilings. Precious marble glowed in the light of a thousand candles. Churches became more elaborate too. Some of the most splendid of all were built in the lands of the Austrian emperor, where architects planned buildings that soared above the landscape, showing the power of emperor and Church together.

Most splendid of all was the monastery of Melk, which stood high on a cliff above the River Danube. The monastery had been there for centuries as a landmark for boats sailing up and down the river. Enriched by its lands, and by the emperor's favour, the monks grew wealthy. So when they decided to rebuild their abbey, they did it in the most magnificent baroque style.

Monasteries had once been simple places where monks devoted themselves to a life of prayer and fasting. Melk was more like a palace. It even had a great room with marble columns and glass chandeliers for the emperor to use as his own. The copper roofs swelled in and out like bells. The dome of the monastery church hung in the sky like a billowing cloud. At Melk the emperor's power and the worship of God combined, and travellers coming down the Danube gasped. The soaring gold and white towers on the cliff seemed to belong not to a humble monastery but to a palace in heaven.

Baroque building became ever more fanciful in the style we now call rococo. But the emperors of Europe didn't only build new churches and palaces. They transformed whole cities. The Pope started it by piercing Rome with long, straight avenues, at the ends of which he placed gates, fountains and obelisks. The czar of Russia, Peter the Great, went even further.

He decided to build a whole city from scratch.

THE CITY ON THE MARSH

St Petersburg, Russia, 1703

For hundreds of years Russia stood apart from the rest of Europe. Its peasants were poor. Its noblemen ignored the latest European fashions and dressed in the traditional Russian way, with heavy coats and long beards.

The Russian emperor, or czar, Peter the Great, was determined to make Russia as powerful and as modern as any other kingdom, so he travelled round the rest of Europe, studying how people lived, how they built ships and houses, and how they managed their governments. Russia seemed shabby when he got home. By comparison with London or Paris, its capital, Moscow, was barely more than a village. So Peter reached a decision. He would build a new capital where the mighty River Neva flows into the Baltic Sea.

Before Peter arrived, the banks of the Neva were lined with reeds and swamps, and herons fished in the shallows. The only buildings were fishermen's cabins, rough structures of tarred planks that looked like wrecked boats. While the fishermen stared in amazement, Peter ordered three great avenues to be laid out across the swamp. They would run from one side of his city to the other, and meet at the heart of his capital. Along each of the avenues were new baroque palaces, and great domes rose into the air. The czar let nothing stand in his way. He didn't have enough stonemasons to build his new city, so he passed a law that no one was allowed to build in stone anywhere else. All over Russia, stonemasons packed their tools and set off for the shores of the Baltic. Prisoners of war were forced to dig trenches. Criminals were put to work draining the marsh. Peter wanted the noblemen who lived in his new capital to be as modern as their palaces, so he even passed laws to make them shave off their beards and put on European clothes. When some of the nobles refused, he charged them a beard tax.

"The money will help pay for my city," he said.

Every day, the czar rode out to watch his new city taking shape. At night he lay in a rough wooden cabin, but rarely slept – he was too busy dreaming up new plans. One day, he told himself, the grandest city in Europe would stand where the waves of the River Neva once washed a deserted shoreline.

Peter the Great didn't live to see his dream come true. But after his death the rulers who followed him went on laying out avenues, palaces and churches on the riverbank. And when the magnificent city was finally complete, they named it after its founder's patron saint: St Petersburg.

Peterhof, the czar's palace by the sea

Peterhof Palace

Menshikov Palace

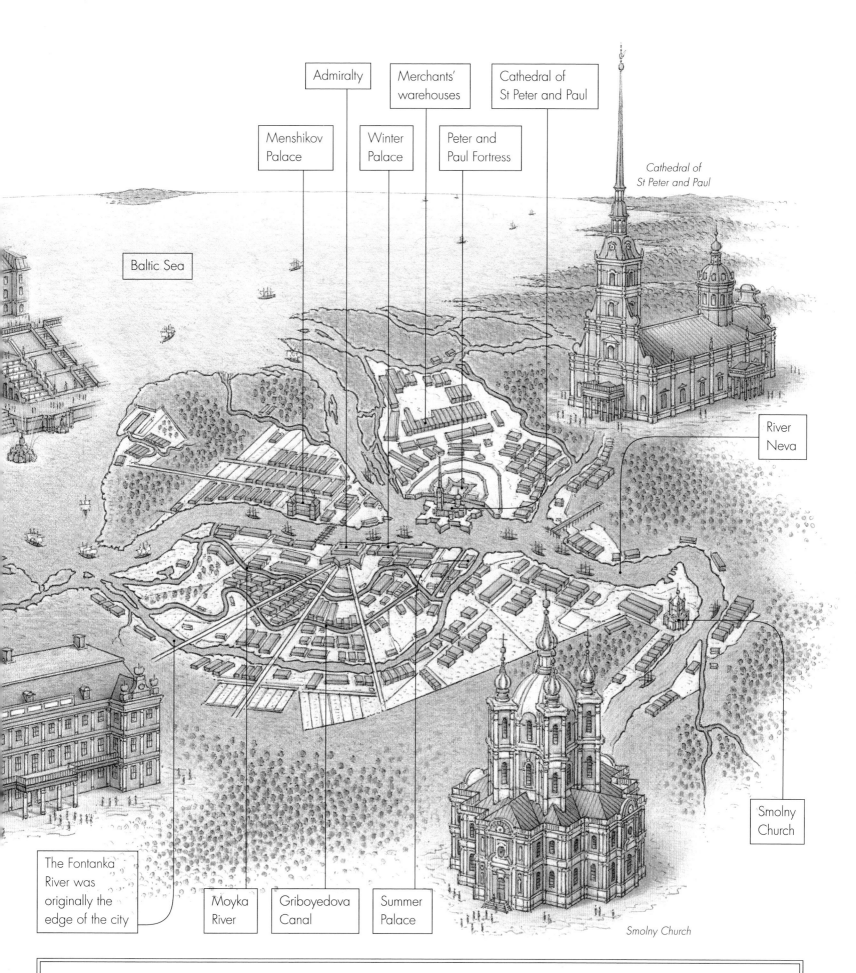

Admiralty

Merchants' warehouses

Cathedral of St Peter and Paul

Menshikov Palace

Winter Palace

Peter and Paul Fortress

Cathedral of St Peter and Paul

Baltic Sea

River Neva

Smolny Church

The Fontanka River was originally the edge of the city

Moyka River

Griboyedova Canal

Summer Palace

Smolny Church

Three great roads or prospekts radiated out from the centre of St Petersburg: Nevsky Prospekt, Voznesensky Prospekt and Gorokhovaya Street

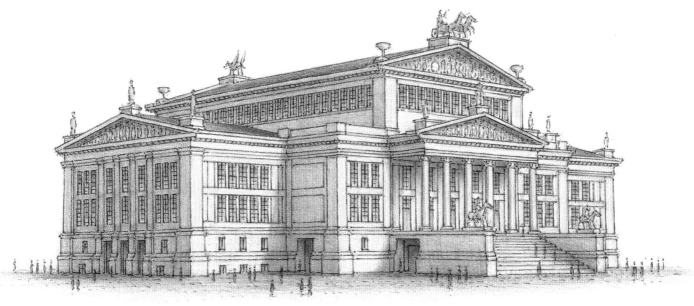

Schauspielhaus, Berlin

LIVING IN THE PAST
From St Petersburg to the Crystal Palace

In Britain, people soon tired of florid baroque buildings. Instead they went back to the simple plans of Andrea Palladio. When kings lost their grip on power in the rest of Europe, baroque fell from favour there too. Instead of inventing something new, designers started to copy styles from hundreds of years before. They copied Palladian villas and Italian palaces from the time of the Renaissance. They copied the ancient ruins that archeologists had begun to dig up in Greece and Egypt. They even started to copy the Gothic style of the Middle Ages.

In Washington the Americans built a beautiful classical home for the president of the United States called the White House, and a classical palace for their parliament, Congress, on Capitol Hill. In Berlin, the capital of Germany, the architect Karl Friedrich Schinkel built an ancient-style concert hall where audiences could hear the music of Mozart and Beethoven amid rows of classical columns. When the British Houses of Parliament burned down in a fire, they were replaced by a medieval-style palace whose bell, Big Ben, rang from a Gothic-style clock tower high above the River Thames. King Ludwig II of Bavaria built himself a fake Gothic castle

The White House, Washington DC

The Houses of Parliament, London

called Neuschwanstein and spent so much time dreaming of the Middle Ages that he went mad.

These different styles were like different suits of clothes put on the same body. The White House looked very different from Britain's Parliament, but in one way they were alike. Their walls were made of brick or stone, and their floors of wood. Their builders expected them to stand for ever, like the great monuments of the past. No one imagined there might be a completely new way of making buildings.

But right at the end of the eighteenth century, people began inventing new ways to make things. Today we call that change the Industrial Revolution. They invented machines to spin thread and weave cloth more quickly. They invented steam engines to drive the machines, and better ways of making iron and steel. Businessmen herded their workers into factories so they could produce things more cheaply. Instead of each craftsman making a chair or table alone, they worked on production lines where one person made the components, another fitted them together and a third varnished them. That way, instead of producing one chair a week, they could make hundreds.

And the Industrial Revolution didn't only change chairs and tables. It changed how buildings were made as well.

Neuschwanstein Castle, Bavaria

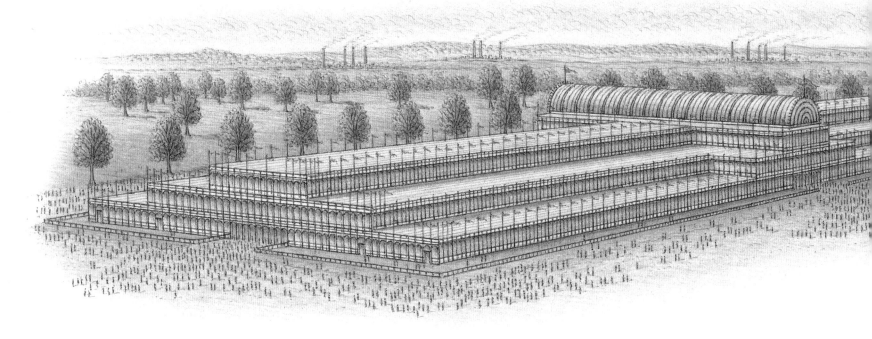

THE PALACE OF GLASS
The Crystal Palace, London, Britain, 1851

Henry Cole, an inventor, and Prince Albert, Queen Victoria's husband, were fascinated by the new way of making things, and saw how rich Britain was becoming as a result. So they decided to hold a great exhibition to display the fabulous things that were being made in British factories. And since by this time Britain ruled India, Canada, Australia and much of Africa as well, they agreed the exhibition would show off the splendours of the British Empire too.

They decided to hold their exhibition in Hyde Park, London, and announced a competition to design the exhibition hall. All the most famous architects in Britain sent in plans. But as they went through the entries, the judges grew more and more worried. The designs showed magnificent palaces decorated with columns and statues, but the exhibition was hardly more than a year away. There would never be time to build any of them.

"Besides," the judges said, "we don't want a stone building that lasts for ever. When the exhibition is over we want to turn Hyde Park back into a park."

Only one designer promised to give them an exhibition hall in time – and one which could be dismantled.

But he wasn't an architect at all. He was a gardener.

His name was Joseph Paxton and he had come up with a new method of constructing greenhouses. Thanks to the Industrial Revolution, machines could make glass in larger panes than ever before. Joseph Paxton had worked out how to get all the panes made the same size, and the iron frames that held them together made to the same pattern, so his greenhouses could be put together quickly and cheaply. To him, making a greenhouse was just like putting together the pieces of a chair.

"I'll make the exhibition hall in the same way," he told the judges.

By the time his design was accepted, the opening date was already drawing near, but because all the parts were made in advance, or pre-fabricated, Paxton was confident everything would be ready. There were no stone walls to build. He didn't need bricklayers or stonemasons. Instead, three hundred thousand sheets

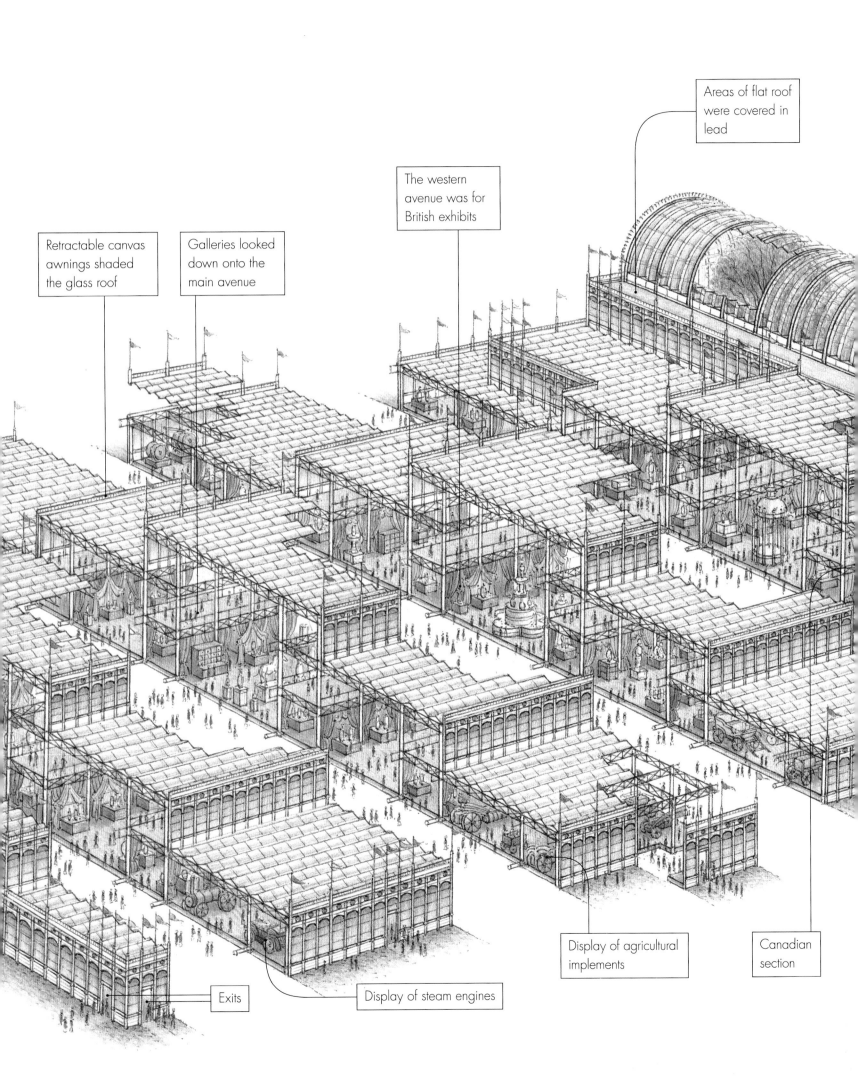

Areas of flat roof were covered in lead

The western avenue was for British exhibits

Retractable canvas awnings shaded the glass roof

Galleries looked down onto the main avenue

Display of agricultural implements

Canadian section

Exits

Display of steam engines

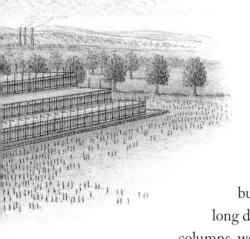

of glass were made at a glassworks in Birmingham and brought to London by the railway – a new invention which made it easier to transport heavy building materials across long distances. A thousand iron columns were cast at forges in the Midlands. In Hyde Park itself, two thousand labourers bolted together the iron and hoisted the glass into place, while steam engines cut the wooden battens that clipped the glass to the frames. There was no muddle about which piece went where, because everything was made to the same pattern. By the day the exhibition was due to open, Paxton's hall was finished.

When Londoners saw its glass vault glinting in the sun, they called it the Crystal Palace. It was so tall that its roof enclosed living trees; so long that its walls stretched as far as the eye could see. Millions came from all over the world to visit the Great Exhibition. They gasped at the wonders inside – furs and carpets, jewels and machines, stuffed animals, pink glass fountains, voting machines, the biggest diamond in the world, pottery, ironwork, perfumes, furniture, pianos, guns, a carved ivory throne, tapestries, silks, sledges, armour,

and a vast lump of gold. But for all the splendour of the exhibits, it was the palace itself people remembered most. Paxton's Crystal Palace wasn't just the biggest building anyone could remember. It was a whole new kind of building, a building not of brick and wood but of metal and glass – a building no one could ever have dreamt of before the Industrial Revolution.

The exhibition only lasted a few months. Afterwards, any other building would have been torn down and its rubble carted away. But the Crystal Palace had been designed so that the pieces could be used again. So the columns, girders and sheets of glass were taken down and carried across the river to a hill in south London. And as they watched the workmen unbolting the iron stanchions and winching the frames down to the ground, people realized that buildings would never be the same again. It wasn't just that they could be made by machines. They *were* machines.

In its new home in south London, Joseph Paxton's exhibition hall lasted for many years; and even though it was eventually destroyed, the area in south London where it stood is still known as Crystal Palace.

From then on, more and more buildings would be made of glass and metal. Instead of being put up in the old way, they would be prefabricated and assembled on site. And they would look like no buildings anyone had made before.

WHERE IT WAS MADE

The factories that made the Crystal Palace were
scattered over Britain. Thanks to railways, the pieces
could be made elsewhere, then brought cheaply to
Hyde Park to be put together. The iron girders were
made by Fox, Henderson and Company, who had
factories not only in London but in Smethwick, near
Birmingham; and Renfrew, in Scotland. The glass
was made in Smethwick by the Chance Brothers.

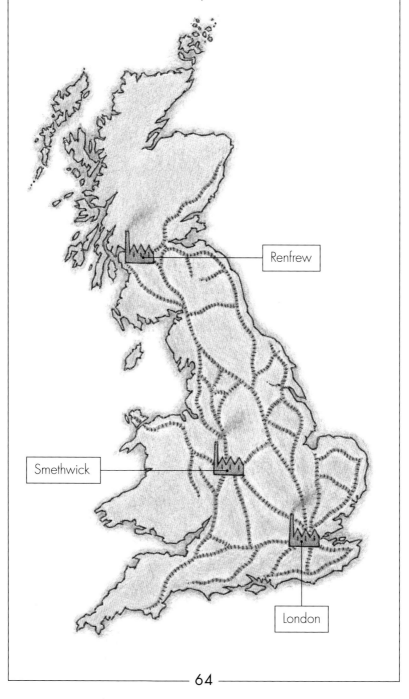

Renfrew

Smethwick

London

The glass roof was divided by gutters. There were twenty-five and a half miles of guttering on the Crystal Palace

Every second column was hollow, to act as a drainpipe

Iron truss girders spanned across the main avenue

Iron columns supported the truss girders

West entrance

Ticket booths

Louvres below the glass let in air

HOW IT WAS PUT TOGETHER

Standard panel of iron and glass

All the cast-iron columns and beams for the Crystal Palace were the same size. There were standard panels for the outside walls as well, and for the semicircular vaults. The builders began by fixing all the cast-iron panels together. The huge ribs of the vault were bolted together on the ground, then lifted into place by cranes. Next, the panes of plate glass were attached to the frame. The workers who fitted them worked from special cradles so they could move quickly along the side of the building – one man managed to fit more than a hundred panes in a single day. The glass was held in place by wooden battens. While the glaziers worked on their cradles, the wooden battens were cut to the right length using power saws driven by steam engines.

Workmen fitting glass into the iron frame

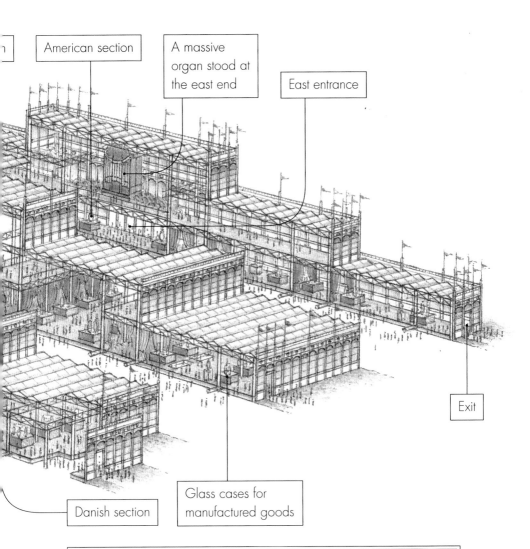

American section

A massive organ stood at the east end

East entrance

Exit

Danish section

Glass cases for manufactured goods

The Crystal Palace was built in only nine months and cost £80,000 (about £6.5 million in today's currency).

The name Crystal Palace was made up by *Punch* magazine.

The building was the first to have public lavatories. Visitors paid a penny to use a toilet called the Retiring Room. That is where we get the phrase 'spend a penny'.

The Great Exhibition in the Crystal Palace gathered more than 10,000 exhibitors from around the world.

Over 13,000 exhibits were on display. Over 6,200,000 visitors came to see them.

The profits from the event paid for the foundation of the Albert Hall, the Science Museum, the Natural History Museum and the Victoria and Albert Museum.

After it was moved to south London, big exhibitions were often staged at the Crystal Palace, including the world's first aeronautical exhibition in 1868 and the first national motor show.

Crystal Palace burnt down on 30 November 1936. 89 fire engines and 400 firemen, half of London's fire brigade, failed to put out the blaze.

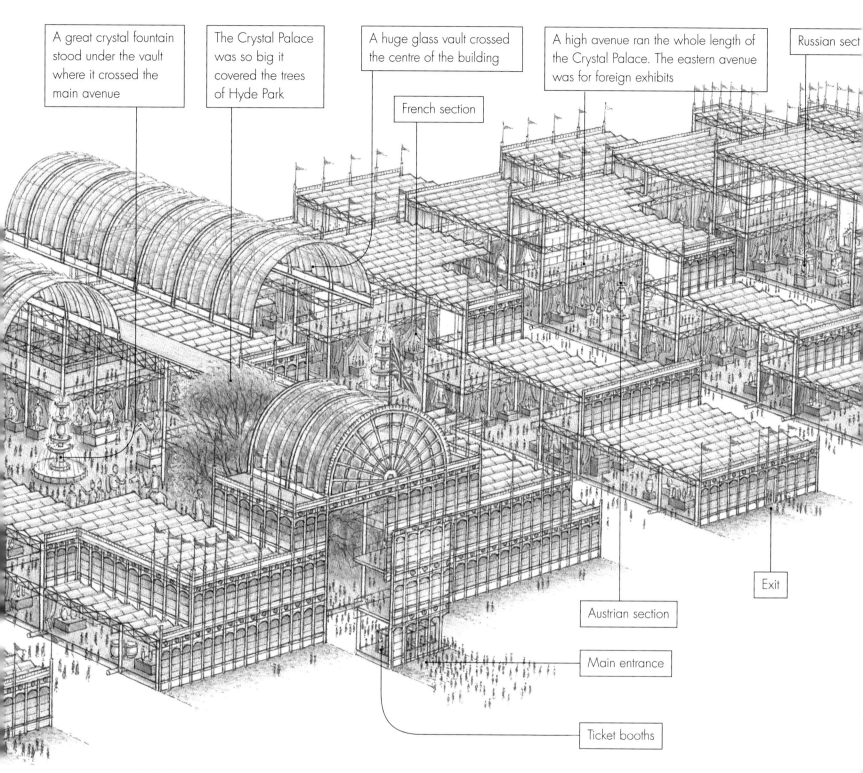

A great crystal fountain stood under the vault where it crossed the main avenue

The Crystal Palace was so big it covered the trees of Hyde Park

A huge glass vault crossed the centre of the building

French section

A high avenue ran the whole length of the Crystal Palace. The eastern avenue was for foreign exhibits

Russian sect

Exit

Austrian section

Main entrance

Ticket booths

THE CRYSTAL PALACE

The great glass palace, full of wonders, proved to millions of visitors that a new age of technology had really begun.

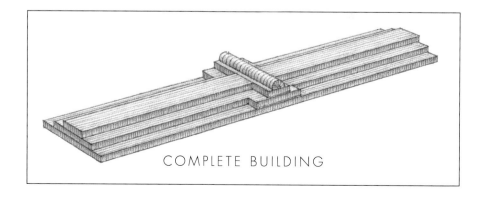

COMPLETE BUILDING

The Red House, Kent

MODERN BUILDINGS
From the Crystal Palace to the Bauhaus

Suddenly all the old rules about buildings looked out of date. The Crystal Palace showed that people didn't have to copy buildings from ancient Greece or Rome, from Egypt or anywhere else.

A British designer called William Morris hated the old rules. Why should buildings be symmetrical? Morris wondered. Why did they need stonework, statues and columns? He looked at the simple houses farmers had been making for centuries. They were just right for their purpose. They were built of plain materials like brick and wood, but were still beautiful. If something was decorated – the front door, for example, or the shelf above a fireplace – it was made plainly and simply by local craftspeople who understood their trade and loved what they did.

That was how buildings should be made, William Morris decided, simply but beautifully, to serve their purpose. He built himself a home in Kent called the Red House to demonstrate what he believed, and started a campaign called the Arts and Crafts Movement to spread his ideas. People were so interested in simple but comfortable Arts and Crafts houses that

Germany even sent an ambassador to Britain to find out more about them.

William Morris and his friends weren't the only ones to be fed up with the old rules of architecture.

"We shouldn't copy old buildings," declared designers in Belgium and France. "We should copy nature!"

So instead of classical columns, pediments and arches, they decorated their buildings with patterns of flowers, leaves and stalks. One of them, Hector Guimard, designed the entrances for Paris's new underground railway, making them from iron that twisted and curled into the shapes of woven leaves. In Barcelona Antoni Gaudí built an apartment block with walls that billowed like trees in a storm, and a fantastical cathedral, the Sagrada Família, with towers that seemed encrusted with flowers.

Other people didn't think buildings needed to be decorated at all.

"Remember the old farmhouses," they said. "If a building serves its purpose, that's enough to make it beautiful."

So they made buildings as simple as possible, planning them as squares or rectangles, covering them with rows of plain windows, and painting them white.

"If you understand what a building is to be used for," they said, "then you'll know how it should look."

Meanwhile, the Industrial Revolution brought more and more change. Factories were being built everywhere. The Greeks and Romans had never built factories, so factory owners couldn't copy them from the monuments of the past. Instead they made them as simply and cheaply as they could, using iron frames and plain brick walls. Next, railways spread all over the world. Copying the past didn't help people build railway stations either. Engineers had to start from scratch when they designed the arching tunnels of metal and glass that covered the platforms and tracks.

At the same time, engineers invented new materials to make buildings with. They cast concrete around steel rods to make reinforced concrete that was as strong as iron but much cheaper. They invented better types of iron as well. For an exhibition in Paris, an engineer called Gustave Eiffel built an iron tower that rose high into the air above the city. Some hated it, but others loved the way the Eiffel Tower

Sagrada Família, Barcelona

soared above the rooftops. Plain structures could be just as beautiful as grand old palaces, they realized. And they became more and more excited by the way new inventions were changing the world. Trains hurried travellers from one country to another in hours. Steamships crossed oceans faster than sailing ships. Aeroplanes whizzed through the skies. The whole world seemed new.

Early in the twentieth century, the First World War killed millions and destroyed whole towns. When it was over there was an even better reason for people to look forward, not back. Those who survived wanted to build a new world rather than remain stuck in the old one. They wanted better homes for poor people. They wanted everyone to share the possibilities of the modern world, with all its wonderful new inventions. Suddenly everything old looked tired and grey. Statues crumbled; stone carvings looked as if they were covered in dust.

"We're living in the modern age," people said. "Everything ought to be modern."

So they set out to invent modern buildings.

Entrance canopy to the Paris Métro

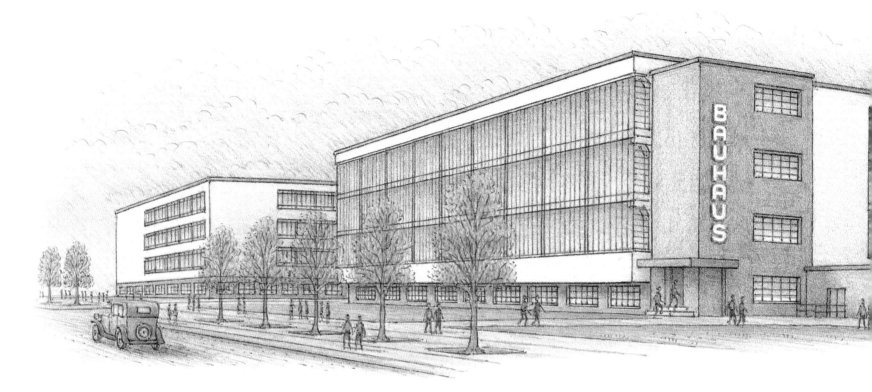

THE SCHOOL FOR BUILDING

The Bauhaus, Dessau, Germany, 1925

Many of the first modern buildings were built in Germany, where designers after the First World War not only questioned what buildings looked like, but who they were for.

In the past, palaces and mansions were built for the rich and for kings and queens. The best buildings were always put up for the most powerful people. Nobody cared where ordinary people lived. Craftsmen made beautiful plates for the rich to eat off, fine fabrics for their curtains and chairs of exotic woods for their dining rooms. Nobody cared what ordinary people ate off, or where they slept at night.

But after the war, designers started to think again. When people came back exhausted from work, wouldn't their lives be easier if there was a scrap of pretty cloth across their window, and a comfortable chair to sit on rather than a rickety old stool? Anyone could enjoy a well-made lamp or a plate with a nice pattern. Wouldn't everybody's life be better if kitchens were safer to cook in and cupboards easier to keep clean? You didn't have to be grand to relax in a comfortable chair.

So designers began to think about the buildings ordinary people lived in.

"Good design shouldn't be about letting the rich show off," they said. "It's there to help everybody."

And they designed factories with huge glass windows to bring the light in, apartment blocks where poor people could live in comfort, and splendid department stores where everyone could buy clothes and furniture.

New buildings, they decided, needed new rules instead of the old classical orders. First they declared that decoration belonged to the past, so modern buildings wouldn't be decorated at all. Next they decided that a building's use should determine how it looked. And finally they agreed it was important to let everyone see the beams and columns that held a building up, rather than hide them behind carvings and ornaments.

"It's more honest," they said.

A group of German designers started a school called the Bauhaus, or Building House, where people could study how to design buildings, carpets, rugs and tables, plates, glasses and cutlery. When designers at the Bauhaus planned a new chair, they didn't care what the chairs of the Greeks and Romans looked like. They experimented with different seats to find the most comfortable, researched new materials, or chose a shape that could be stored conveniently. If they made a coffee pot, they looked for a handle that would lift comfortably and a spout that poured without dribbling. By this method, Bauhaus students designed kitchens that were easier to cook in, lights that were better to read by, and jugs, rugs, tables and cloths that could make everyone's homes more comfortable.

But there was one thing the Bauhaus's director, Walter Gropius, still dreamt of.

"We need to show everyone what a modern building should really look like," he said.

So when the Bauhaus moved to Dessau, east of Berlin, he and his partners set out to design the Bauhaus a new home.

The new building was divided into three blocks: one for the students to live in, one for workshops and one for the classrooms. Each block was designed to suit its purpose, so the students' rooms had rows of balconies where they could relax from their work, and the workshops had huge walls of glass to bring in light. All the walls were clean and white. There were no classical columns or carvings at the Bauhaus. It was simple and beautiful in the way that ships or trains are beautiful – because it suited its purpose.

Excitedly the students poured into their new rooms and set up their tools in the workshops. They planned to design a new world where everything was beautiful and everything was made for its purpose – just like their new home. At the Bauhaus, everything seemed possible.

Unfortunately the school was to last only a few years. A new ruler, Adolf Hitler, took over Germany. He and his followers, the Nazis, hated everything the Bauhaus stood for. The Nazis weren't interested in people's comfort or convenience; they didn't want brighter factories or better homes for ordinary people. They wanted buildings to show their strength and scare their enemies. So instead of homes and shops, they built porticoes they could drape with the Nazi banner, and stadiums where vast crowds could chant Hitler's name; they built balconies Hitler could make speeches from, and wide avenues where his soldiers could march in procession. They were determined to crush the little white Bauhaus, whose students designed kitchens and chairs to help people live comfortably.

So the Bauhaus was closed down, the students packed their bags and left, and workmen arrived to block up the glass walls of the workshops. The dream of the Bauhaus seemed to be over.

But it wasn't. The school itself might have been closed, but its ideas had spread all over the world.

THE BAUHAUS

Each wing of the Bauhaus –
for workshops, classrooms and
living quarters – was designed
to suit its purpose.

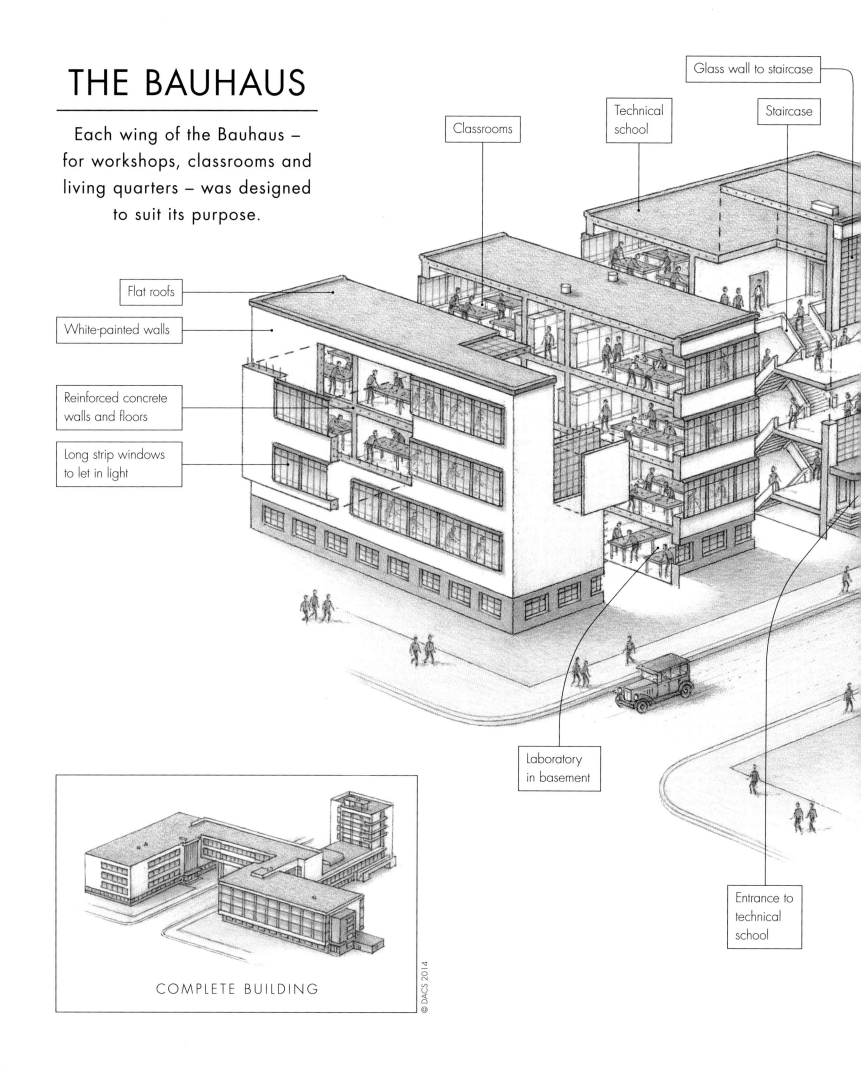

Glass wall to staircase

Staircase

Technical school

Classrooms

Flat roofs

White-painted walls

Reinforced concrete walls and floors

Long strip windows to let in light

Laboratory in basement

Entrance to technical school

COMPLETE BUILDING

© DACS 2014

REINFORCED CONCRETE

Concrete is very strong, so it is just the right material for columns, and for the foundations a building rests on. But if you made a beam of concrete and rested it on two walls, it would soon crack in the middle. That is because columns and beams have to be strong in different ways. Columns are compressed. Beams are stretched. Concrete is good at being compressed but bad at being stretched.

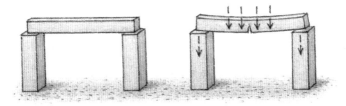

Ordinary concrete makes good supports but bad beams

Reinforced concrete solves the problem. To make it, builders put steel rods inside the moulds they have prepared, then pour the concrete around them. With steel rods inside it, concrete is almost as good at being stretched as steel, while the rods make it stronger at carrying crushing weights than ever. Reinforced concrete is one of the best materials for making frames, floors, walls and domes. It can be poured into any shape and resist almost any force.

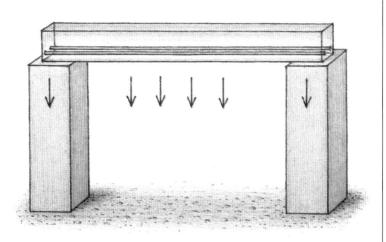

Reinforced concrete beam

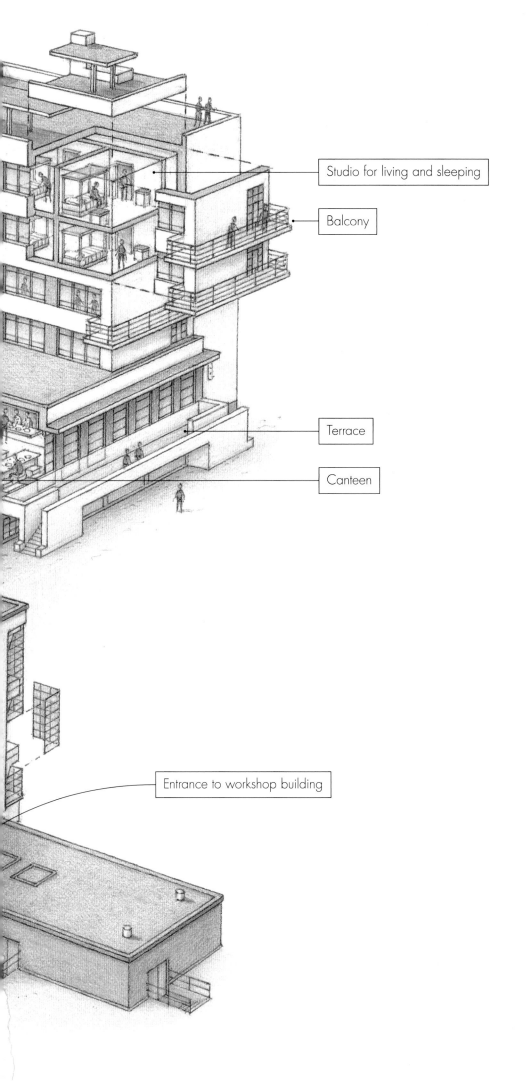

Studio for living and sleeping

Balcony

Terrace

Canteen

Entrance to workshop building

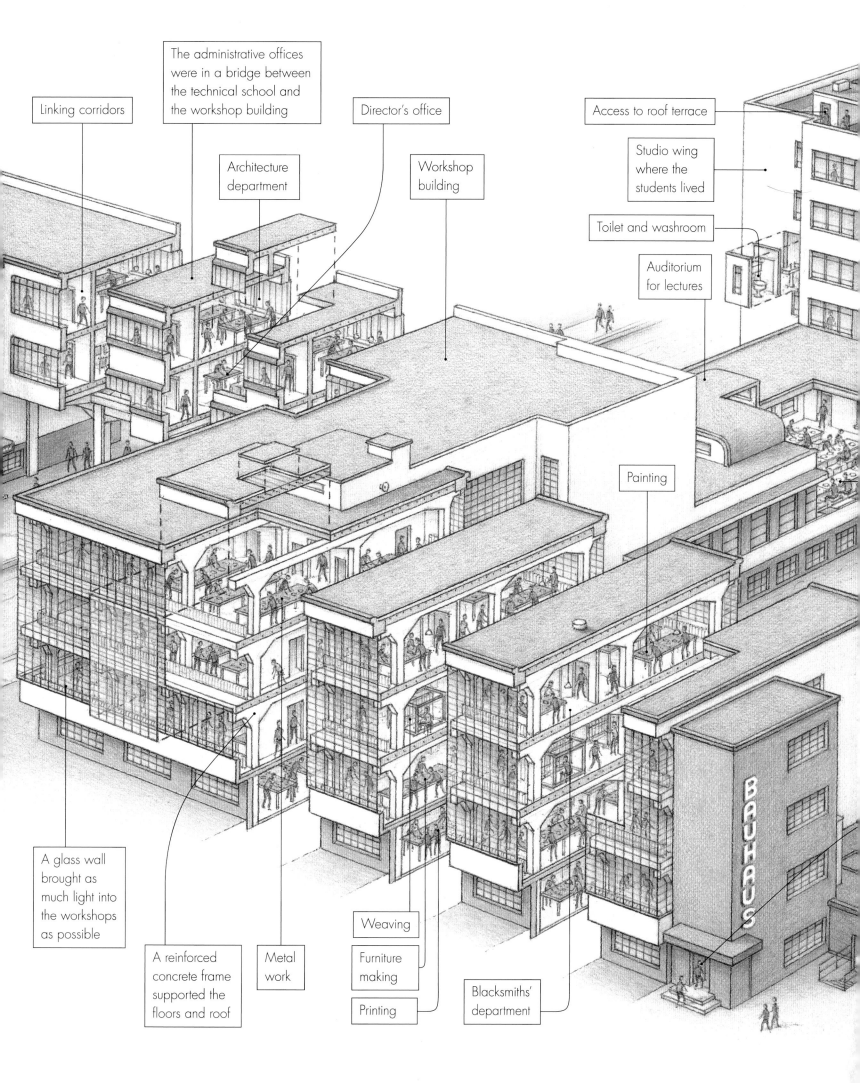

Linking corridors

The administrative offices were in a bridge between the technical school and the workshop building

Director's office

Access to roof terrace

Architecture department

Workshop building

Studio wing where the students lived

Toilet and washroom

Auditorium for lectures

Painting

A glass wall brought as much light into the workshops as possible

A reinforced concrete frame supported the floors and roof

Metal work

Weaving

Furniture making

Printing

Blacksmiths' department

BAUHAUS

AMERICA

From the Bauhaus to the Chrysler Building

Many of the teachers from the Bauhaus fled abroad to escape the Nazis. Ludwig Mies van der Rohe, its last director, went to America.

America was the perfect place to find out what a new world should look like: it *was* a new world. There were no classical ruins, no palaces, no dusty Gothic cathedrals. Its towns weren't full of narrow streets left over from the Middle Ages; they were laid out in broad, even grids. Railways criss-crossed the continent, aeroplanes soared over it and motor cars rolled in their thousands from vast new factories in Chicago and Detroit.

Like everyone else, the Americans had begun by copying the old rules for buildings, but they were eager to try out new ideas. An architect called Frank Lloyd Wright started experimenting with houses that were simple and comfortable, like the houses William

Johnson Wax Building, Wisconsin

Morris and his friends made in England. He lived on the plains of the Midwest, and as he watched the endless prairie horizon, he drew houses so low and flat they almost seemed part of the landscape around them. The plains seemed to flow through them, sweeping away walls until kitchen, living and dining rooms merged into one. Frank Lloyd Wright built a house over a waterfall that seemed to grow out of the rock itself, its balconies soaring over the cliff edge while water foamed below them.

America was full of large companies, so Frank Lloyd Wright was employed to build offices too. For the Johnson Wax Company he designed a great hall whose columns spread across its ceiling like water lilies. It was only an office building where ordinary people worked day after day, but to them it seemed as beautiful as any cathedral.

American buildings grew larger, thanks to new inventions. In the past, buildings couldn't be too wide, because everyone had to sit near a window to write a letter or read a report. Thanks to electric light offices could become much bigger. In the past, buildings couldn't be very tall because no one could face climbing too many flights of stairs. After Elisha Otis invented a safe electric elevator, the sky was the limit.

Louis Sullivan, Frank Lloyd Wright's teacher, started putting up tall buildings in Chicago. They

Fallingwater, Pennsylvania

were constructed from steel frames with panels of stone or concrete bolted to the outside, and they towered over passers-by.

"Skyscrapers!" people said when they looked up.

Skyscrapers were the first truly American buildings. They showed everyone how bold America was. They showed that while Europe, damaged by the First World War, was sinking into the past, America was the future. The Nazis took over Germany. People all over Europe felt old and tired. But the Americans didn't. And they started a new competition: to make the tallest building in the world.

REACH FOR THE SKY

The Chrysler Building, New York, USA, 1928

Americans liked to boast that anyone in their country could get rich. Someone could start a new business and within months it could be worth millions. And of all the businesses in America, the richest, fastest-growing and most exciting of all was making cars. Cars were a recent invention, and Americans loved them so much that within just ten years Ford and General Motors had become two of the biggest companies in America.

Walter Chrysler had started a business making cars and dreamt that the Chrysler Corporation would grow just as big as Ford and General Motors. So when he announced a new headquarters in New York City, he was determined to make a building the world would sit up and take notice of – not a stuffy old stone palace, but something as new, dynamic and beautiful as his cars. It would be the tallest skyscraper in the world.

At that time, the tallest structure in the world was the Eiffel Tower in Paris, which was 300 metres high. But the Eiffel Tower wasn't really a building – you couldn't live or work in it. The tallest building was the Woolworth Building in New York City, 241 metres high, from whose viewing platform visitors could see the city spread out below them, the hills inland and liners far out on the ocean. Chrysler wanted his skyscraper to be even taller. He studied the plans with his architects, then announced that his new building would reach 246 metres into the air.

But Walter Chrysler wasn't the only person planning the tallest building in the world. One day a messenger rushed into his office with the news that the Bank of Manhattan had started a skyscraper on Wall Street that would be 68 storeys high – 14 metres taller than the Chrysler Building. Chrysler summoned his architects and builders to an emergency meeting. Together they added extra floors to the plans and raised the Chrysler Building to 282 metres – 22 metres higher than the Bank of Manhattan.

Walter Chrysler gave orders for work to continue without rest until the tower was finished. Day and night, workmen laboured on the scaffold, hauling huge steel beams into the air, bolting them into place and fixing metal panels to the outside. The Chrysler Tower rose at the rate of four storeys every week. But on Wall Street the Bank of Manhattan was going up even faster. And then its owners revealed a secret plan. Although they had promised a height of 68 storeys, they had secretly added an extra three. In May 1930 they announced that they had finished the tallest building in the world. Flags were hung from the new skyscraper while car horns blared and Wall Street erupted in cheering.

But Walter Chrysler didn't give up. He had a secret plan of his own. The Bank of Manhattan tower was 283 metres high – one metre taller than his own building – but inside the Chrysler Building, his men had assembled a stainless steel spire. At the last minute they winched it into place and when the Chrysler Building opened, a few weeks later, its peak soared 319 metres above the street. The Chrysler Building wasn't just taller than the Bank of Manhattan, but higher even than the Eiffel Tower. It was the tallest structure on earth.

Walter Chrysler's triumph didn't last long. Even before his tower opened, work had started on the Empire State Building, which soon overtook it, rising 381 metres to its roof. But the Chrysler Building wasn't just special because it was tall. Walter Chrysler had wanted his building to delight people as much as his cars did. So the corners of the upper floors were decorated with eagles copied from the ornaments on his car bonnets, the lift doors were inlaid with flowing patterns of metal and wood, and the crown of the tower rose to the clouds in arches of stainless steel that glinted in the New York sunlight.

Walter Chrysler's skyscraper may not have stayed the tallest tower in the world. But he had made sure it would be the most beautiful.

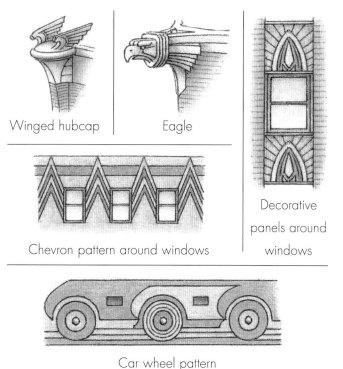

Winged hubcap Eagle

Chevron pattern around windows

Decorative panels around windows

Car wheel pattern

Decorations used on the skyscraper

COMPLETE BUILDING

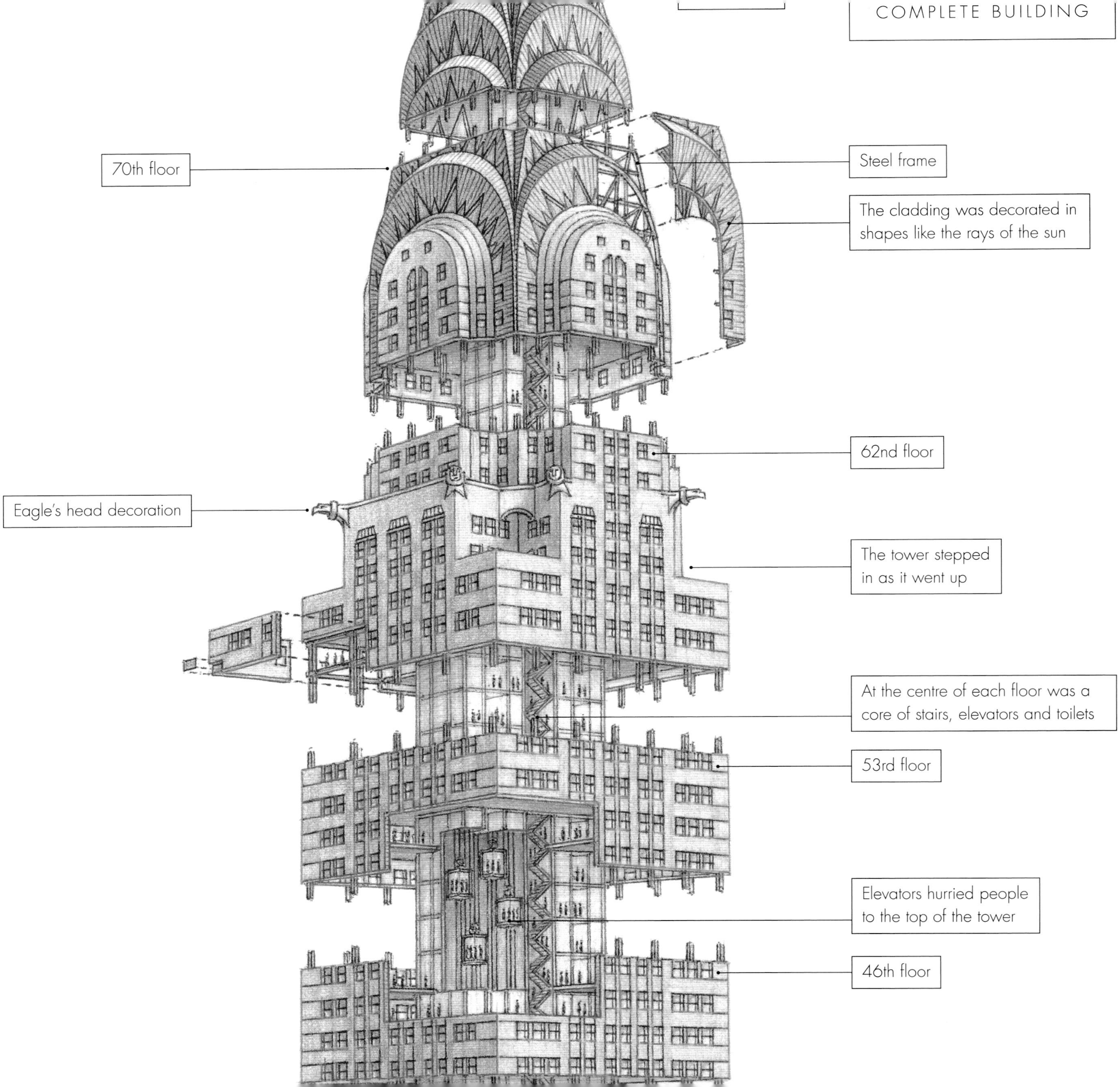

Steel frame

The cladding was decorated in
shapes like the rays of the sun

62nd floor

The tower stepped
in as it went up

At the centre of each floor was a
core of stairs, elevators and toilets

53rd floor

Elevators hurried people
to the top of the tower

46th floor

70th floor

Eagle's head decoration

The Chrysler Building contains 20,961 tons of steel, 391,881 rivets, 3,826,000 bricks, 10,000 light bulbs and 3,862 windows.

It has 32 elevators, all of them inlaid with precious woods from around the world.

It is still the tallest brick building in the world.

It was the first fully air conditioned skyscraper.

More than 750 miles of electrical conductor wire were used in the construction, equivalent to the distance from New York City to Chicago.

Walter Chrysler refused to pay his architect, William Van Alen, who had to sue him to get any money for designing the tower.

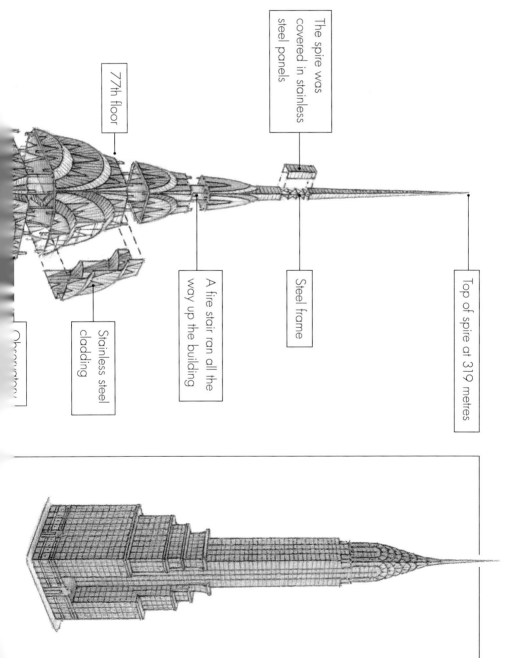

The spire was covered in stainless steel panels

77th floor

Steel frame

A fire stair ran all the way up the building

Stainless steel cladding

Top of spire at 319 metres

Observatory

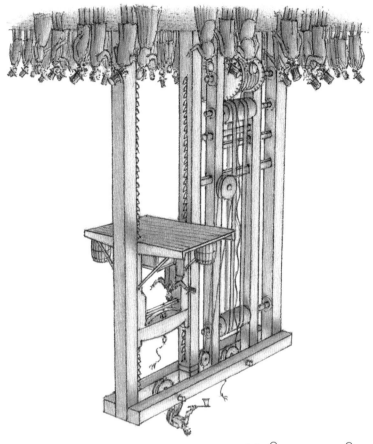

OTIS'S SAFETY ELEVATOR

A long time ago, people invented ropes and pulleys to hoist heavy weights up and down on platforms. The ropes were sometimes pulled by horses. Quite often they broke, and the platform tumbled all the way to the ground. The invention of powerful engines meant platforms – or even little cabins – could be pulled high into the sky. But nobody wanted to travel on them.

What would happen if the rope broke? Elisha Otis invented an automatic brake that would keep people safe even if it did. He demonstrated it at the World's Fair in 1854, three years after the Crystal Palace was built. Standing on a platform high above the ground, he ordered an assistant to cut the cable with an axe. Everyone gasped as the cable parted, but Elisha Otis's safety elevator didn't fall to the ground. After that, people were happy to travel in lifts, and buildings rose higher and higher.

SKYSCRAPERS

Deciding on the official height of a tall building is harder than it sounds. Should spires be included? Or antennae? Should measurements be taken from the roof or the highest floor? In the case of the Willis Tower the antenna masts are not architectural features so its height is measured from its roof, while the spires of the Petronas Twin Towers are counted as architectural features. So though the Willis Tower appears taller, its official height is 10 metres lower than that of the Petronas Twin Towers.

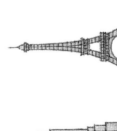

SAQQARA
62m

PYRAMID
OF CHEOPS
146m

CHRYSLER
BUILDING
319m

EIFFEL TOWER
324m
spire added in 1957

EMPIRE STATE
BUILDING
381m

WILLIS
TOWER
442m

PETRONAS TWIN
TOWERS
452m

TAIPEI WORLD
TRADE CENTRE
509m

BURJ
KHALIFA
830m

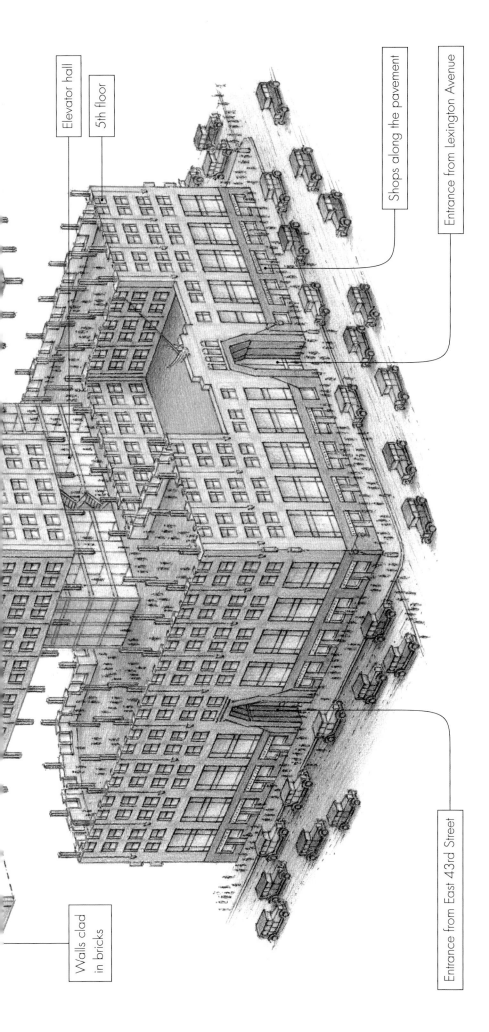

Elevator hall

5th floor

Shops along the pavement

Entrance from Lexington Avenue

Walls clad
in bricks

Entrance from East 43rd Street

THE CHRYSLER BUILDING

For centuries people had dreamed of reaching the sky. The Chrysler tower soared higher than any building before it.

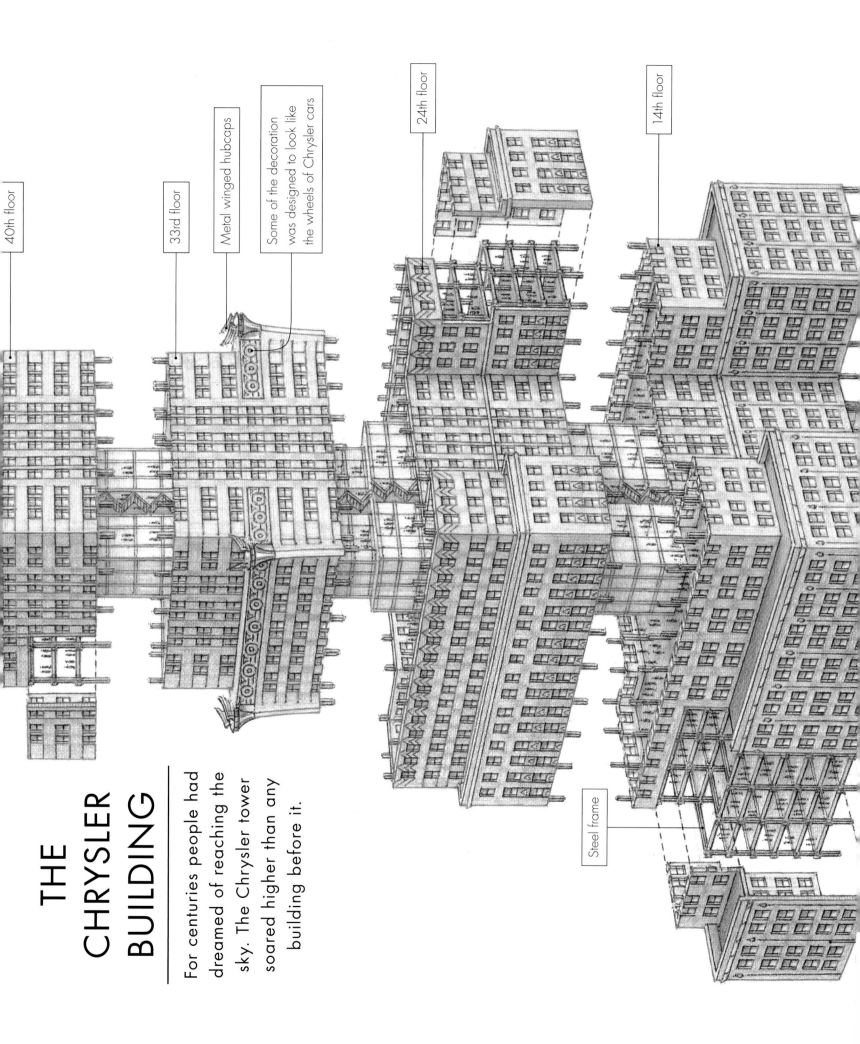

40th floor

33rd floor

Metal winged hubcaps

Some of the decoration was designed to look like the wheels of Chrysler cars

24th floor

14th floor

Steel frame

THE INTERNATIONAL STYLE
From the Chrysler Building to the Sydney Opera House

Everyone who passed the Chrysler Building stopped to stare up at its shining sides, at the zigzag windows on the crown and the spire soaring into the clouds. But some architects hated it.

What had happened, they wondered, to the idea that buildings should be simple and undecorated? Didn't decoration belong to the past? Shouldn't structure be displayed, not hidden? Some architects wanted to have fixed rules for making buildings. And two years after the Chrysler Building opened, they held an exhibition in New York City to explain them.

Buildings should be simple in shape, they declared. They shouldn't have any ornament. They should suit their purpose and be built honestly out of modern materials like concrete and steel, so you could see how they were made. Most of all, since everything was now made by machines, buildings should be thought of as machines too – machines for living and working in. They called their rules the International Style and demanded that everyone should follow them. There was no room in their exhibition for the Chrysler Building because it was covered in decoration. There was hardly room for Frank Lloyd Wright and his prairie houses.

To start with, modern architecture had been exciting. With the old rules for buildings forgotten, people had found all kinds of things to inspire them: the rushing lines of a train, how a factory worked, or the flat prairie horizon. Buildings could look however they wanted. There were new materials to make them from. There were so many different ways of building that each could be just right for its own time and place, for the people who built it and the men and women who were going to use it. But now it looked as if modern architecture was to be governed by yet another set of rules.

Some of the buildings in the New York exhibition were very beautiful. Mies van der Rohe had designed a pavilion in Barcelona, Spain, that seemed almost

Mies van der Rohe's Barcelona Pavilion, Barcelona

like a sculpture. But not everyone liked the idea that buildings had to follow rules. After all, the people who lived in them weren't all the same. They wanted buildings that were special to them, buildings that told stories. The only story the International Style told was about machines.

Meanwhile in Germany, Adolf Hitler and the Nazis were growing more and more powerful. They took over Austria and attacked Czechoslovakia, Poland, France and Russia. Hitler's allies, the Japanese, attacked America. Soon the whole world was at war.

Since the last great war had ended, engineers had invented aeroplanes that could fly over enemy cities and drop bombs to destroy them. In London, air raid sirens wailed and people hurried to take shelter as the streets shook with explosions and flames devoured office blocks, homes, shops and cinemas. Soon British and American bombers flew over German cities, destroying houses, blocks of flats, factories and ancient churches. By the time the war ended, hardly a building was left standing in Berlin. The Americans dropped two nuclear bombs on Japan that flattened the cities of Hiroshima and Nagasaki as if they had never existed.

Millions of people lost their homes. They needed to work, but there were no offices to work in. They needed new machines, but there were no factories to make them in. It felt as if the whole world had to be built again.

And so the governments of Europe rebuilt their ruined cities in the International Style, which was the quickest and cheapest way to build. As cities in Africa and Asia grew, they were built in the International Style

Alvar Aalto's Finnish Pavilion, New York

too. All over the world, tall, square, concrete buildings appeared, and glass office blocks rose into the sky.

Some people tried to do things differently, though. In Finland a designer called Alvar Aalto made buildings that felt special for the people who used them. They were made not just of concrete and steel but of wood and brick as well. Alvar Aalto, and others like him, wanted to use their imagination, rather than follow rules. They wanted buildings to be beautiful, not just cheap and efficient.

And when the city of Sydney, in Australia, decided to build an opera house, one architect got the chance to show just how beautiful a building could be.

THE ARCHITECT'S SKETCH
The Sydney Opera House, Sydney, Australia, 1959

Sydney stands on green hills around a deep blue harbour where gulls call and waves crash against the cliffs. The site chosen for the opera house was down by the harbour shore, where a spit of land thrust into the sea at Bennelong Point. From the surrounding hills, the new opera house would look as if the whole city was wheeling around it.

The mayor of Sydney announced a competition for the design of the opera house. From all over the world, crates of drawings and models arrived. One by one they were opened and the judges pored over them. But when they had finished examining the entries they felt strangely disappointed. Most of them had been full of diagrams showing how the opera house would work – how the tiers of seating would rise, and the bars and ticket offices fit together; how they would build storerooms for the scenery, dressing rooms for actors, and practice rooms for singers to prepare in. But the judges weren't looking for storerooms. They were looking for a building they could imagine on the shore of Sydney Harbour, with the blue ocean at its feet and the green hills behind it. And they didn't see that in any of the entries – except for one.

The entry they liked best wasn't filled with diagrams and plans. What caught the judges' attention was a simple little sketch in pen and ink. Wondering, they passed it from hand to hand. It seemed to show sails hovering on the harbour shore – or perhaps they were the wings of birds that had just come to land. The lines of the sketch danced in front of the judges' eyes. Would the scenery fit in? Would the actors get from their dressing rooms to the stage? Suddenly those things didn't seem to matter so much. The little sketch wasn't a building made of concrete and steel. It was a poem.

No one was even sure how it would be built, but the judges couldn't get it out of their minds, and at last they proclaimed the architect who drew it, a young Dane called Jørn Utzon, the winner.

They had no idea then how many years would pass, how many bitter arguments would follow, before the Sydney Opera House was built.

Centuries earlier, builders had had to invent new ways

NEW STRUCTURES

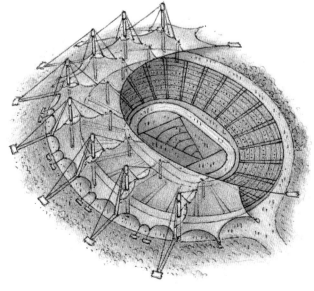

The Sydney Opera House wasn't the only building for which new kinds of structure were invented. As engineers learnt how structures worked, and invented calculations to design them more accurately, they came up with more and more exciting shapes. A designer called Buckminster Fuller patented the geodesic dome, which used tiny lengths of steel to enclose a massive sphere.

Geodesic dome

Engineers soon realized that structures suspended from masts could be much lighter than structures resting on columns on the ground, and invented networks of steel cable that could be hoisted into place to act as roofs. For the Olympic Games in 1972, the German engineer Frei Otto designed a stadium of hanging cables woven together like a gigantic spider's web.

Olympic Stadium, Munich

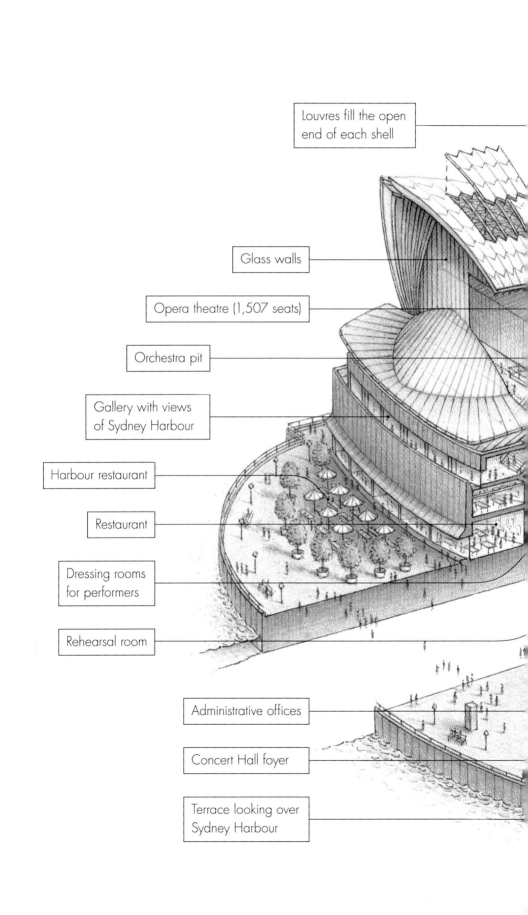

Louvres fill the open end of each shell

Glass walls

Opera theatre (1,507 seats)

Orchestra pit

Gallery with views of Sydney Harbour

Harbour restaurant

Restaurant

Dressing rooms for performers

Rehearsal room

Administrative offices

Concert Hall foyer

Terrace looking over Sydney Harbour

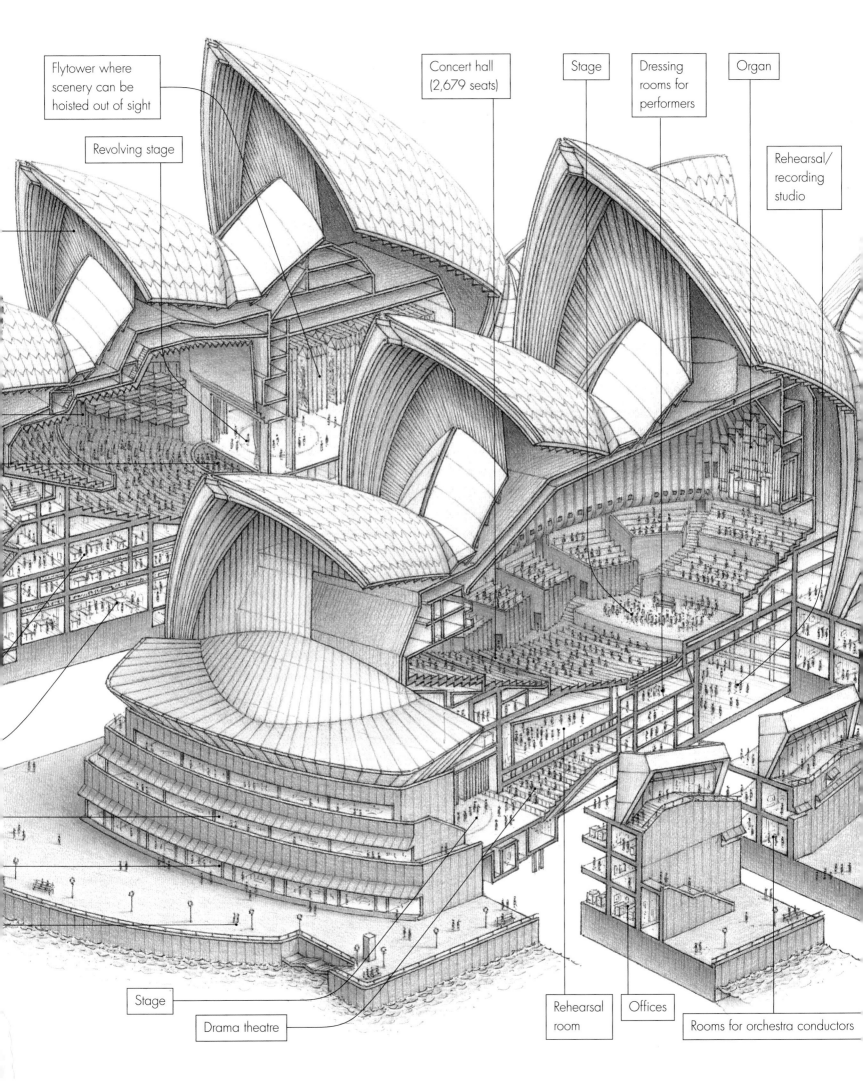

Flytower where scenery can be hoisted out of sight

Revolving stage

Concert hall (2,679 seats)

Stage

Dressing rooms for performers

Organ

Rehearsal/ recording studio

Stage

Drama theatre

Rehearsal room

Offices

Rooms for orchestra conductors

of making arches and vaults to raise Gothic cathedrals like Notre-Dame. Designing Sydney Opera House was just as hard. How were the delicate sails Jørn Utzon had sketched to be turned into a real building? The engineers used computers to calculate the curve of each wing, but the wings were all different shapes and no one could work out how to make moulds for the concrete. They solved that problem by making all the wings from different pieces of the same sphere. Then they came up with a way to make each sphere from concrete ribs, like the ribs of a Gothic cathedral. But no one had ever built a building like Sydney Opera House before, and every challenge they faced was new. How would they lift the ribs into place? How would they fix them together? Months went by, then years, as models were made, and plans drawn, torn up and

drawn again. Still the designers worked. Still the design wasn't finished. In the Middle Ages, townspeople sometimes took a hundred years to finish their cathedral. To the people of Sydney, it felt as if their opera house was taking just as long.

Meanwhile, the cost kept going up, and it wasn't long before people started to blame one another for the delay. Jørn Utzon blamed the city's politicians; they blamed him. After a terrible row, he was dismissed and flew back to Denmark in fury.

So Jørn Utzon, who had drawn the little sketch of sails floating on the water, wasn't there on the day the opera house finally opened. Sydney Harbour was packed with boats, the shore lined with people, and the hills crowded with sightseers. On Bennelong Point the roofs of the opera house glinted in the sunshine. They looked exactly as they had in Jørn Utzon's drawing – like the wings of birds that had just landed on the shore. And finally everyone understood why he had designed it that way. Jørn Utzon had realized that because Sydney surrounded it on every side, the opera house couldn't have a front, a back or a roof. It was like a sculpture; it had to be beautiful from every direction.

Utzon never visited his opera house. Years later, the people of Sydney asked him to visit, but by then he was too sick. He had one comfort, though. His opera house had become one of the most famous buildings in the world. And it was always there in Jørn Utzon's mind.

"He is too old by now to take the long flight to Australia," his son wrote. *"But as its creator he just has to close his eyes to see it."*

THE SYDNEY OPERA HOUSE

The Opera House's roofs seemed to hover effortlessly above the shore, but building it took years of ingenuity.

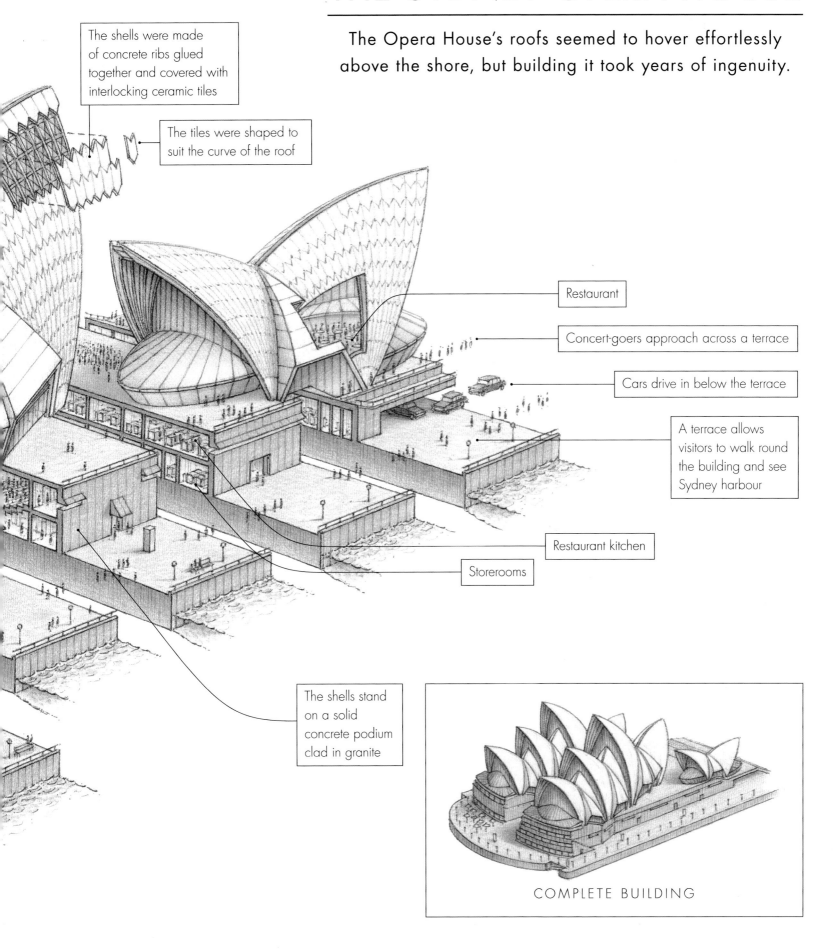

The shells were made of concrete ribs glued together and covered with interlocking ceramic tiles

The tiles were shaped to suit the curve of the roof

Restaurant

Concert-goers approach across a terrace

Cars drive in below the terrace

A terrace allows visitors to walk round the building and see Sydney harbour

Restaurant kitchen

Storerooms

The shells stand on a solid concrete podium clad in granite

COMPLETE BUILDING

TIME FOR A CHANGE
The Pompidou Centre, Paris, France, 1971

The Sydney Opera House proved something that the builders of Gothic cathedrals had discovered centuries before: a great building can transform a whole city, making people throng to visit it and changing the way they think about it. Four years after the Sydney Opera House opened, Paris was also transformed by an extraordinary new building.

After it was finished, the first visitors to the new arts centre in the Beaubourg district had no idea what to make of it.

"They've forgotten to take the scaffolding off," said one.

"It's inside out," said another. "They've put all the pipes and wires on the outside!"

But one thing everyone agreed on: the Pompidou Centre didn't look like a building at all. It had no front and no walls. Instead, huge steel columns rose above the square outside, supporting massive brackets and giant bits of machinery interlaced with moving escalators. It almost looked as if a huge spacecraft had crash-landed in the middle of Paris.

It had been the president of France's idea to build a new arts centre in Paris. Paris was the most elegant city in the world, with graceful stone buildings, wide boulevards, gardens full of fountains and museums full of masterpieces, but President Pompidou wanted something different.

"Paris needs to wake up," he said. "It isn't just a historic city. It's a place full of new ideas as well, so it should have an arts centre where artists can meet and work together." And he announced a competition to design it.

Most of the world's great architects entered, but the competition was won by two young architects from Britain and Italy, Richard Rogers and Renzo Piano, who had never built a large building before.

Before starting work, they had spent a lot of time looking at drawings of museums in architecture books. They had bought books about Paris and studied its beautiful buildings. But everything in the books seemed frozen in time. The museums were made of stone. The streets were made of stone. It seemed as if the only reason people

through them, vast ducts for heating, and miles of wiring for lights and electrical sockets. All that machinery would need to be replaced and mended, so it made no sense to bury it inside the building. Rogers and Piano put it on the outside, where everyone could get at it.

That wasn't all. The new arts centre was there to help people share ideas, so the best thing to put on the outside was people and ideas: escalators and walkways to carry people; huge screens to display ideas. So much the better if the Pompidou Centre kept moving and changing. That was the whole point of modern art: it was always shifting and coming up with something new. People in the past had wanted their buildings to remain unchanged for centuries but the Pompidou Centre would be different. As technology and ideas changed, the Pompidou Centre would change as well. It didn't matter to Rogers and Piano that their arts centre looked more like a machine than a building. That was what it was: a machine for art.

Many of the first visitors were baffled as they watched people rising up the outside escalators and hanging over the balustrades.

"Where are the steps?" they asked. "Where's the grand entrance?"

Younger people loved it, though. They bought tickets for the escalators, met in the café on the roof and looked down on the stately roofs of Paris.

And it was when people stared across Paris at the towers of Notre-Dame Cathedral that they finally realized how special the new Pompidou Centre was. Centuries before, Bishop Maurice had ignored old rules to make something completely new. The Pompidou Centre looked nothing like Notre-Dame Cathedral, but Richard Rogers and Renzo Piano had done the same thing. Like Notre-Dame, their building was completely different from any that had gone before.

made buildings was so that they would last for ever.

But maybe lasting for ever wasn't the most important thing in the world. The world Rogers and Piano knew wasn't stuck in stone; it was constantly changing. Telephones transmitted messages in the blink of an eye. Computers made calculations in microseconds. Just two years before, a rocket had taken men to the moon. Their parents had never known television; now every home had a screen. People didn't look at frozen pictures any more; they looked at moving images.

So shouldn't they make a different kind of building for this different kind of world? Not a heavy building of stone that was fixed for ever, but a light building, a young building, a building for a world of computers and screens, of constant change and movement.

You could never tell what artists would do next, they decided, so there was no point dividing the arts centre into galleries and rooms. The best thing was to make huge empty floors that people could split up, change and use exactly as they chose. So they put all the columns on the outside, leaving nothing inside to clutter up the space.

Modern buildings need huge machines to pump air

THE POMPIDOU CENTRE

The Pompidou Centre was like no museum or gallery that had ever been built before. It looked more like a machine than a building.

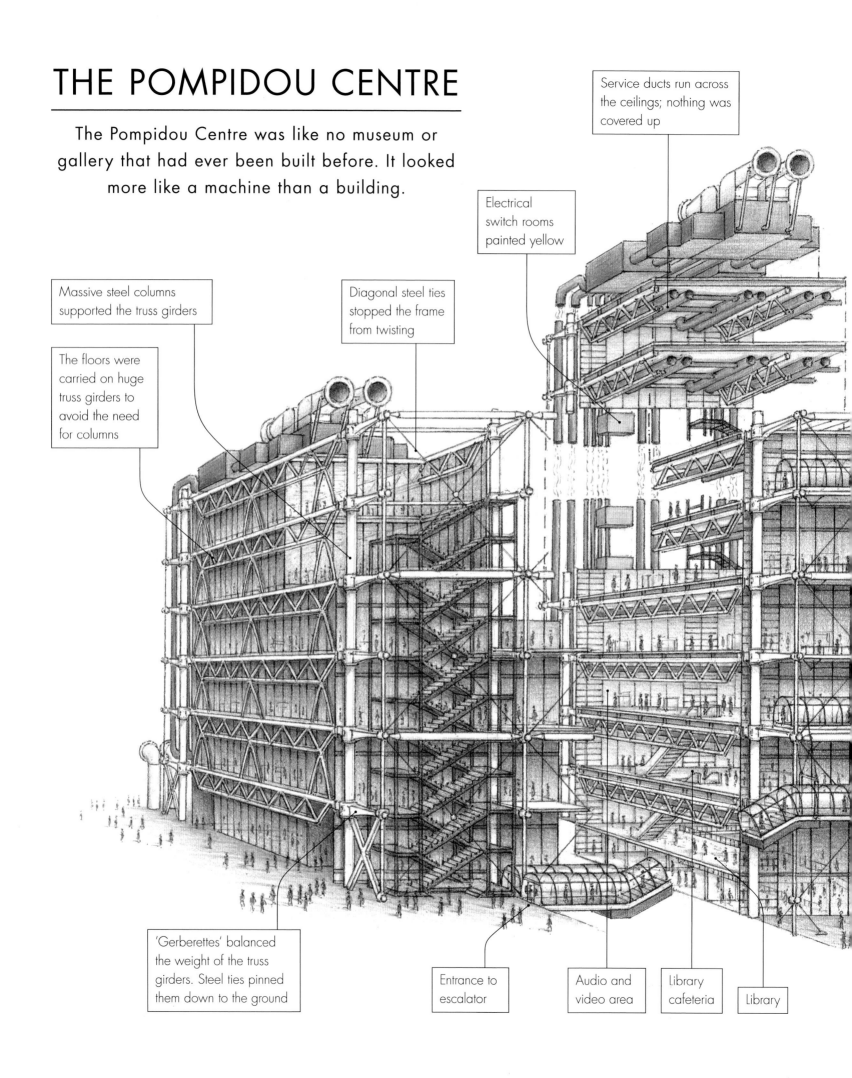

Service ducts run across the ceilings; nothing was covered up

Electrical switch rooms painted yellow

Massive steel columns supported the truss girders

Diagonal steel ties stopped the frame from twisting

The floors were carried on huge truss girders to avoid the need for columns

'Gerberettes' balanced the weight of the truss girders. Steel ties pinned them down to the ground

Entrance to escalator

Audio and video area

Library cafeteria

Library

WATER, AIR, POWER AND LIGHT

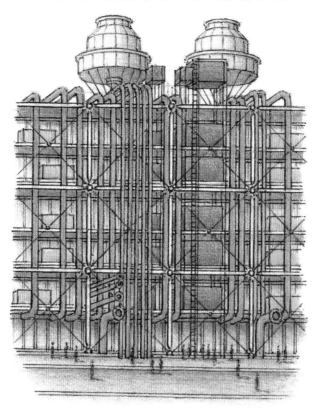

Services at the Pompidou Centre

In the old days buildings were lit by windows and heated by fires. Water came from a well outside. Buildings today are quite different. Water is pumped to every room that needs it – and waste pumped out again. Miles of cable take power and computer data from room to room, while electric lights burn brightly even at night. Fans pump in warmed air in winter and chilled air in summer. These days, the services that bring water, air, power and light into buildings are as important as the beams and columns that hold them up.

At the Pompidou Centre the designers put the services on the outside and gave each one its own colour. Water pipes are green and air ducts blue, while pipes holding electrical cables are painted yellow. Everything painted red is to do with escalators, lifts, safety alarms and fire escapes.

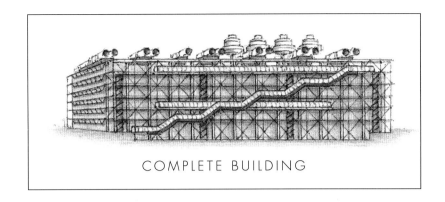

COMPLETE BUILDING

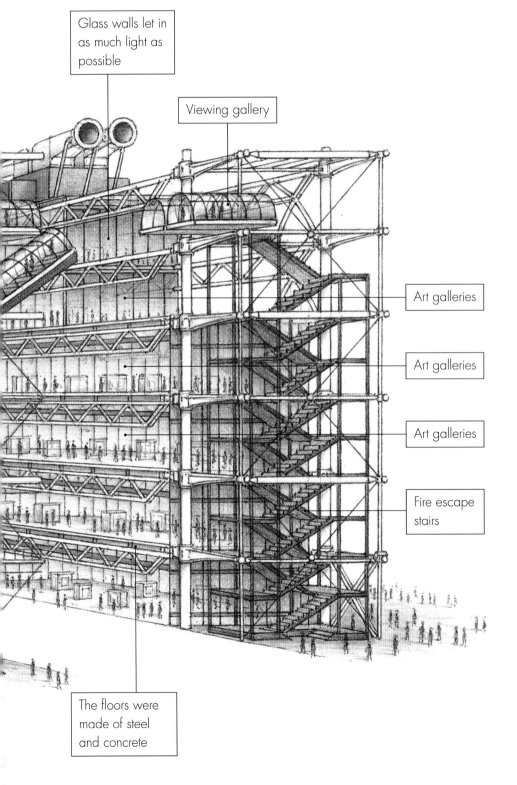

Glass walls let in as much light as possible

Viewing gallery

Art galleries

Art galleries

Art galleries

Fire escape stairs

The floors were made of steel and concrete

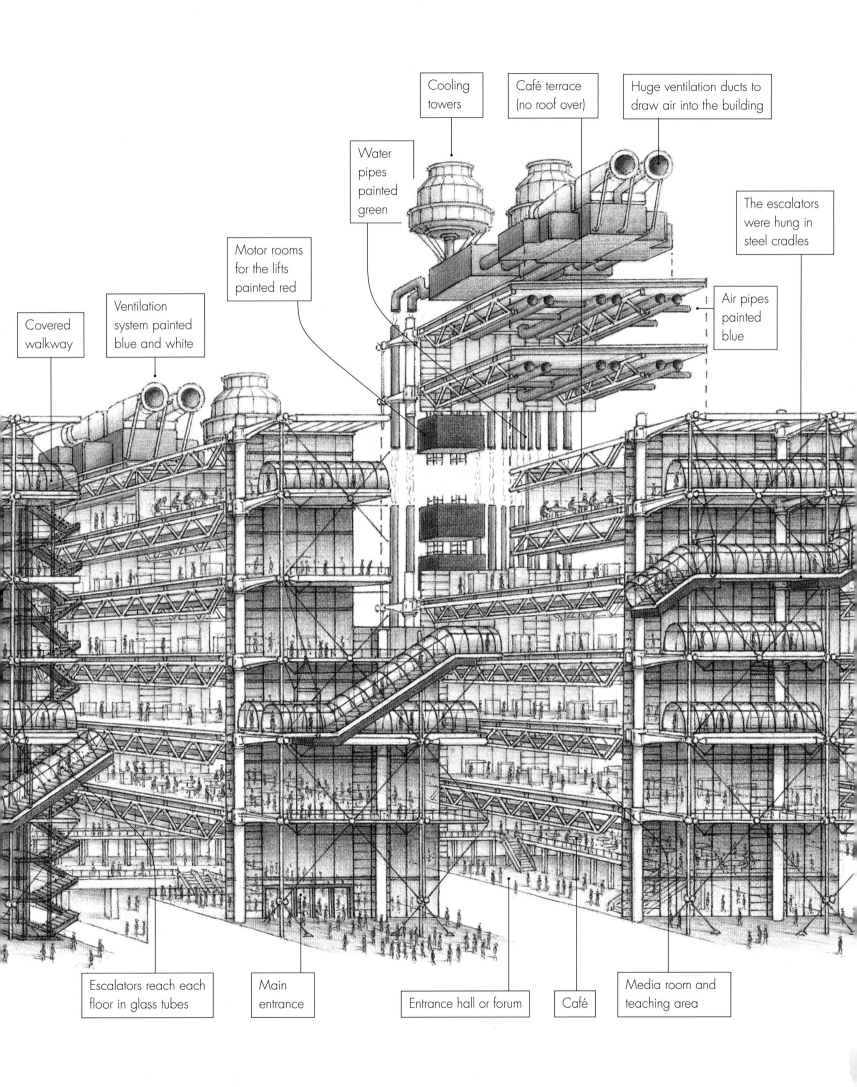

Cooling towers

Café terrace (no roof over)

Huge ventilation ducts to draw air into the building

Water pipes painted green

The escalators were hung in steel cradles

Motor rooms for the lifts painted red

Air pipes painted blue

Covered walkway

Ventilation system painted blue and white

Escalators reach each floor in glass tubes

Main entrance

Entrance hall or forum

Café

Media room and teaching area

THINK BEFORE YOU BUILD

The Straw Bale House, London, Britain, 2001

From Pharaoh Djoser's tomb at Saqqara to the Pompidou Centre in Paris, people have spent fortunes on buildings, and used all their ingenuity to make them beautiful and strong. Buildings have displayed the might of kings and the wealth of the rich; sometimes they have demonstrated complicated theories; sometimes they have given us a glimpse of heaven. But all buildings start with the questions the first builders had to ask when they looked round the forest, wondering how to find shelter. What do we want the building for? And what materials have we got to make it from?

Today we need to ask some new questions as well.

People in the past didn't stop to think when they cut down trees to make a house: the forests stretched for thousands of miles. They didn't have to worry about running out of stone or clay, while lighting a fire to bake bricks hardly made a stain in the blue, empty air. It seemed as if there would be enough materials to last for ever, and no amount of fires would damage the sky. But these days the earth doesn't seem so strong. Cities grow larger and larger, while people cut down forests faster than the trees can grow. All over the world, factories roll steel beams and giant machines crush cement. The new houses we build need energy to heat and light them, so boilers devour gas and pylons stretch across the countryside. Every city on earth burns with a million electric lights.

Today we have to learn to make buildings that harm the earth less.

Sarah Wigglesworth and her partner, Jeremy Till, were architects who needed a home and a place to work. First they had to find somewhere to build it, so they searched London until they stumbled on an empty forge near a railway track. Then they started planning their house.

They talked about the houses they had imagined when they were children: of towers where you could sit and dream; of bedrooms so snug you would fall asleep as soon as you lay down. Most of all, they discussed how they could stop the house from using too much energy. They decided to make the south side as open as possible, to take light from the sun, while the walls on the north stayed thick and warm. To take away heat in summer they would build a tower that rose high above the roofs – and the tower would be a place to sit and look out across London. They would build a cool larder instead of having a fridge, gather rain from the roofs to flush their toilets, and leave a big empty space under the house where they could keep chickens and grow vegetables. They didn't cut down the trees in the yard. They wanted to live among them like birds.

When it was time to start building, they gathered rubble in wire baskets to act as foundations and cut up old railway sleepers to make window frames. They shredded old newspapers for insulation to keep the house as warm as possible.

They wanted to make their own bricks, but they didn't have a kiln, so they piled up sandbags to make the wall next to the railway tracks. And they bought straw bales from a farmer and stacked them up as a wall for the bedrooms and kitchen.

When the building was finished it didn't look like anyone else's house, with its tower, sandbags and straw bales, and its roof covered in grass and flowers like a hillside. But Sarah Wigglesworth and Jeremy Till had done what people have been doing ever since they started making buildings. They had built a shelter from the best materials they could find – just as the first people had done in the forests or mountains. And like all the best buildings, their house told a story. It was a story about thinking before you build; about learning how to make homes that don't damage the earth, so that people in the future can go on making buildings and living in them, just as the very first people did when they piled wood against wood to make shelter for the night.

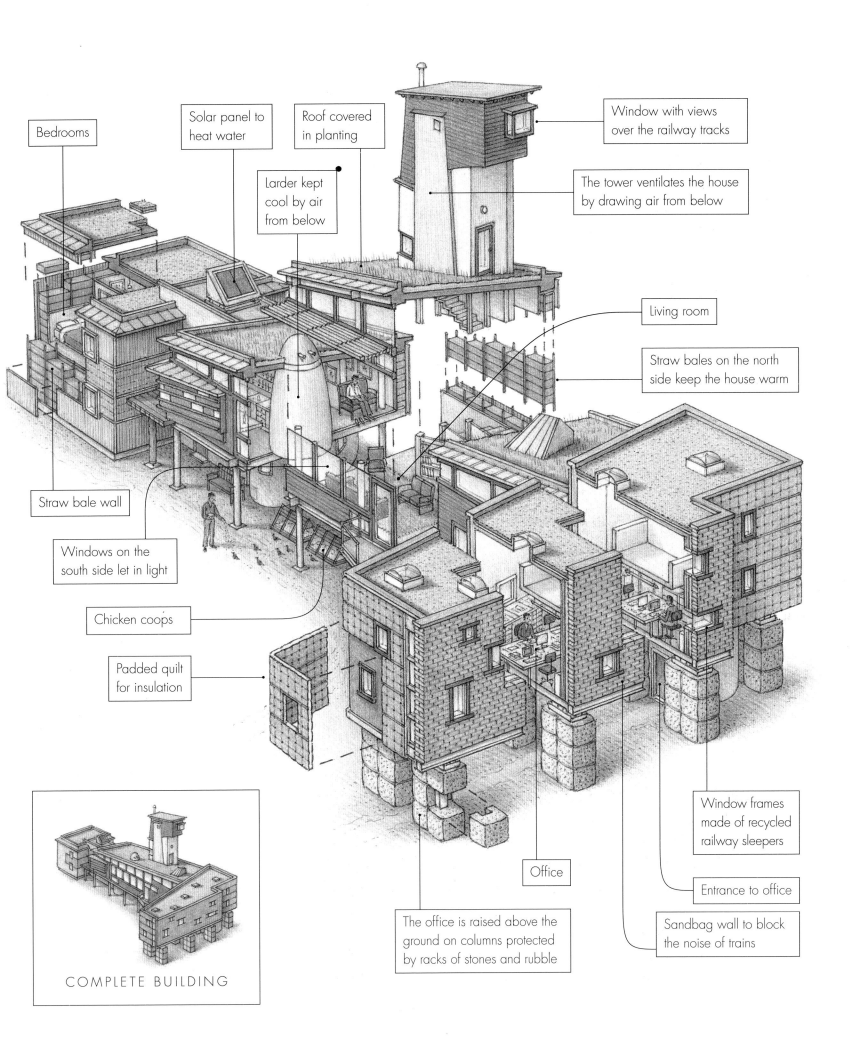

Bedrooms

Solar panel to heat water

Roof covered in planting

Larder kept cool by air from below

Window with views over the railway tracks

The tower ventilates the house by drawing air from below

Living room

Straw bales on the north side keep the house warm

Straw bale wall

Windows on the south side let in light

Chicken coops

Padded quilt for insulation

Window frames made of recycled railway sleepers

Office

Entrance to office

The office is raised above the ground on columns protected by racks of stones and rubble

Sandbag wall to block the noise of trains

COMPLETE BUILDING

INDEX & TIMELINE

From the ancient world to the early Middle Ages

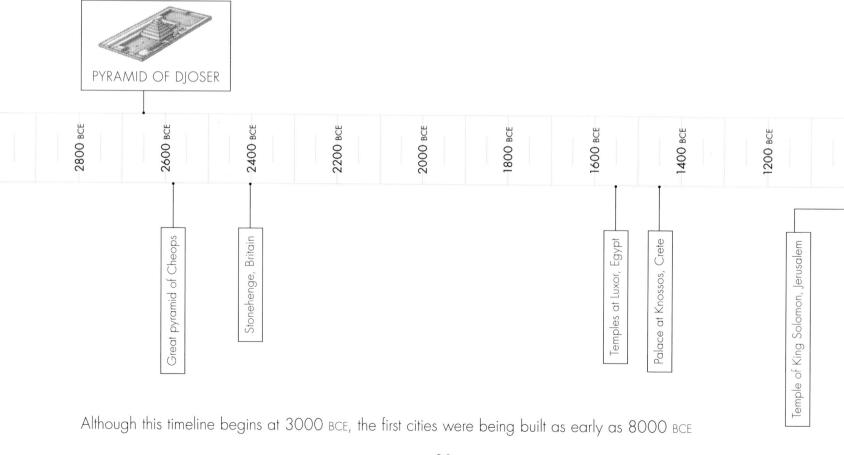

PYRAMID OF DJOSER

2800 BCE 2600 BCE 2400 BCE 2200 BCE 2000 BCE 1800 BCE 1600 BCE 1400 BCE 1200 BCE 1000 BCE

Great pyramid of Cheops

Stonehenge, Britain

Temples at Luxor, Egypt

Palace at Knossos, Crete

Temple of King Solomon, Jerusalem

Although this timeline begins at 3000 BCE, the first cities were being built as early as 8000 BCE

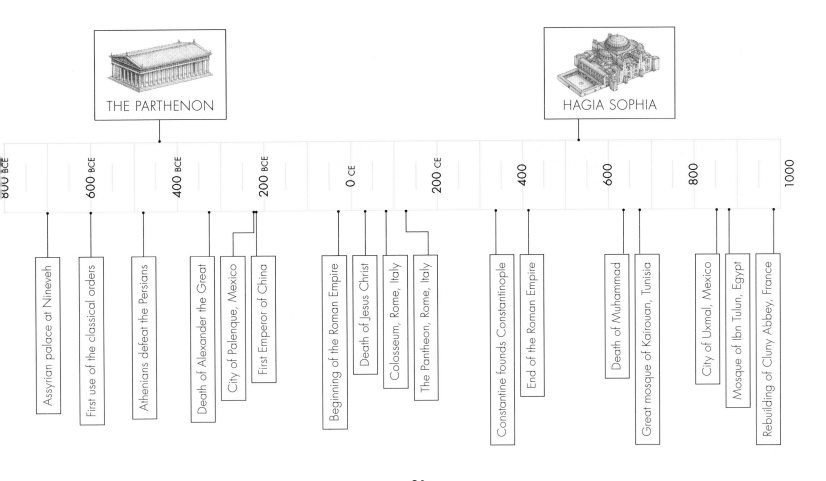

The Middle Ages

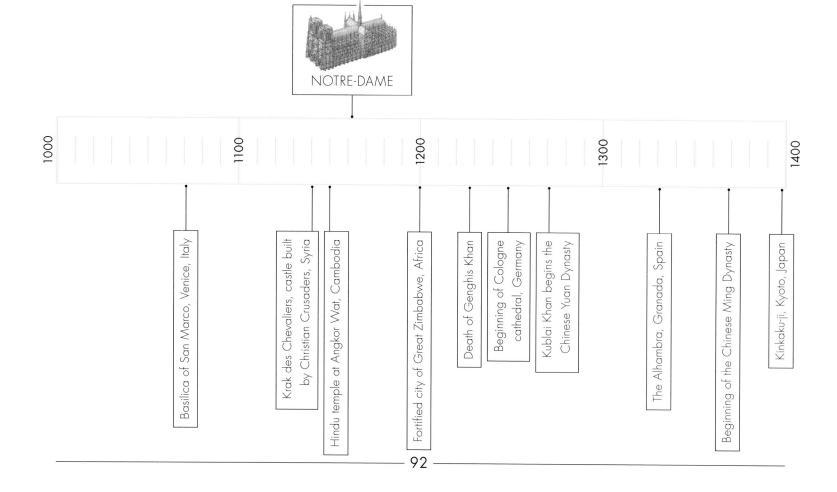

NOTRE-DAME

1000   1100   1200   1300   1400

Basilica of San Marco, Venice, Italy

Krak des Chevaliers, castle built by Christian Crusaders, Syria

Hindu temple at Angkor Wat, Cambodia

Fortified city of Great Zimbabwe, Africa

Death of Genghis Khan

Beginning of Cologne cathedral, Germany

Kublai Khan begins the Chinese Yuan Dynasty

The Alhambra, Granada, Spain

Beginning of the Chinese Ming Dynasty

Kinkaku-ji, Kyoto, Japan

The Renaissance and the Baroque

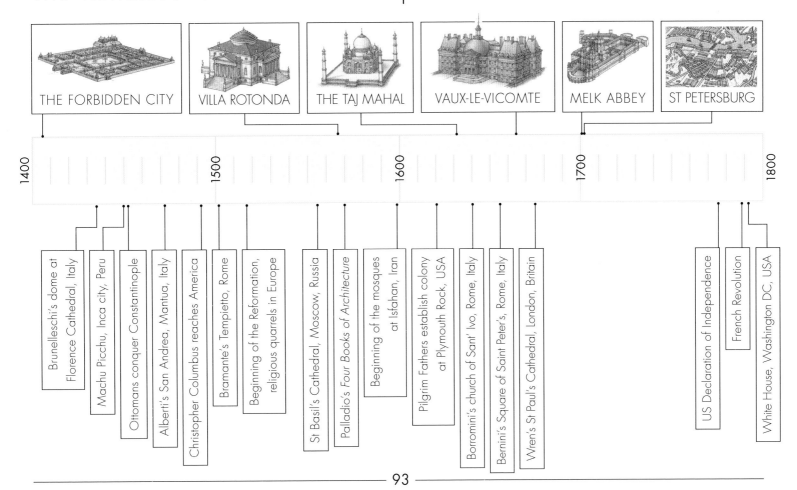

The Nineteenth Century

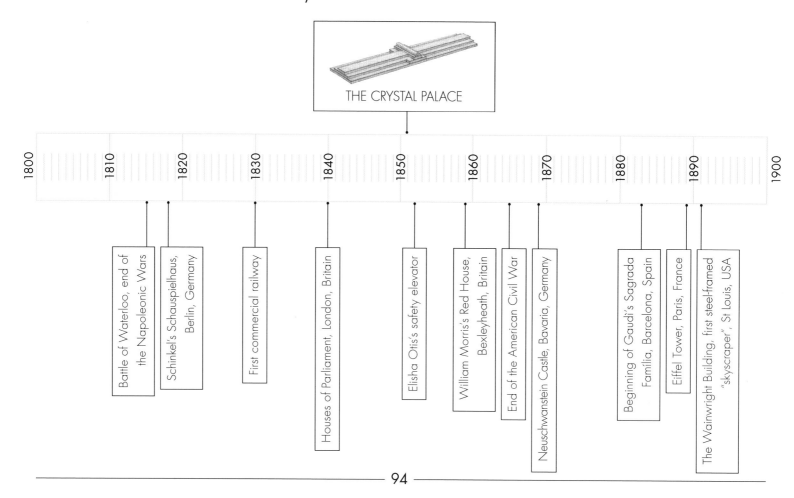

THE CRYSTAL PALACE

1800
1810
1820
1830
1840
1850
1860
1870
1880
1890
1900

Battle of Waterloo, end of the Napoleonic Wars

Schinkel's Schauspielhaus, Berlin, Germany

First commercial railway

Houses of Parliament, London, Britain

Elisha Otis's safety elevator

William Morris's Red House, Bexleyheath, Britain

End of the American Civil War

Neuschwanstein Castle, Bavaria, Germany

Beginning of Gaudí's Sagrada Família, Barcelona, Spain

Eiffel Tower, Paris, France

The Wainwright Building, first steel-framed "skyscraper", St Louis, USA

ACKNOWLEDGEMENTS

I'd like to thank my agent,
Andrew Lownie, Caz, Alice, Ben
and everyone else at Walker,
who've made the book such
fun to work on, the ever-helpful
staff of the Yearsley–Richards
    Research Forum, my wife
    Nicola, and my children,
    Martha and Joe, who love
    visiting Gothic cathedrals
    even more than I do. P.D.

*The publisher gratefully acknowledges
permission for the reproduction of the
following buildings:* The Bauhaus,
DACS; The Chrysler Building, Rubenstein
Corporations; Fallingwater and interior
of the Johnson Wax Company, CMG
Worldwide; German Pavilion, Mies Van
der Rohe Foundation; Finnish Pavilion,
Alvar Aalto Foundation; Munich Olympic
Stadium, Frei Otto Foundation; Sydney
Opera House, Sydney Opera House. *Every
reasonable effort has been made to trace
ownership of and/or secure permission for
the use of copyrighted material. If notified
of any omission, the editors and publisher
will gladly make any necessary corrections
in future printings.*

The Twentieth Century and beyond

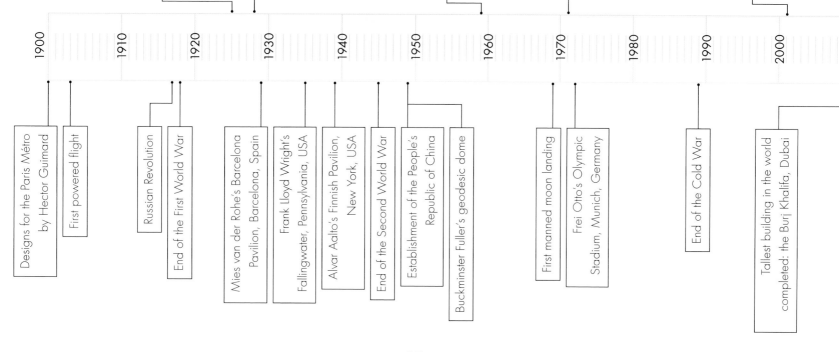

THE BAUHAUS

THE CHRYSLER BUILDING

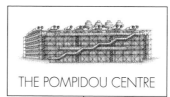
SYDNEY OPERA HOUSE

THE POMPIDOU CENTRE

THE STRAW BALE HOUSE

1900 — 1910 — 1920 — 1930 — 1940 — 1950 — 1960 — 1970 — 1980 — 1990 — 2000 — 2010

Designs for the Paris Métro by Hector Guimard

First powered flight

Russian Revolution

End of the First World War

Mies van der Rohe's Barcelona Pavilion, Barcelona, Spain

Frank Lloyd Wright's Fallingwater, Pennsylvania, USA

Alvar Aalto's Finnish Pavilion, New York, USA

End of the Second World War

Establishment of the People's Republic of China

Buckminster Fuller's geodesic dome

First manned moon landing

Frei Otto's Olympic Stadium, Munich, Germany

End of the Cold War

Tallest building in the world completed: the Burj Khalifa, Dubai